Close Me If You Can

The A to Z of Maximizing Your Sales Opportunities to Retail
Buyers

©2012

Thomas Spago

ISBN 978-1-300-02898-7

Table of Contents

Introduction

Introduction

I am a buyer. Depending on the retailer or industry our rare breed is also referred to as a category manager, merchandise manager, purchasing manager and perhaps some good or not-so-good pet names by the sales community. I have over a decade of buying experience in portfolios over two hundred million dollars at two of the largest multi-billion dollar retailers in North America.

And I am about to let you into my head.

I will expose you to everything you need to know about buyers – how we think, how our business operates, what we want from you (the salesperson) and what concerns us about people on the other side of the desk - so you can use this knowledge to your advantage. Of course it's not like I'm a magician breaking the magician's code and divulging how to do all the big Vegas show illusions, but it is fairly rare that you will ever get this far inside the buyer's world and be able to use that golden knowledge to raise your game to new levels.

I have had plenty of success. I have been highly recognized for my strategies, analytical skills, organization and market share growth, and I have also been in the game a long time – not only in buying but also many other areas of the retail business that you will also need to know. I am fortunate enough to have worked with some great buyers, replenishment people, senior executives, marketing gurus and other key roles in the buying cycle. I have also worked with some incredible salespeople and executives that have made my job and life much easier. I will leverage the knowledge of many of these people in the book and have also pulled in representatives of some of North America's largest manufacturers and suppliers who have given me their own insight and challenges so that I can speak to this in the pages ahead.

The commentary I provide in the pages ahead may sound complex or may be extremely simple, but I am calling out behaviours and situations I have encountered for the purpose of giving you guidance on what works, and what may not, when maximizing your opportunities selling to buyers in various retail segments. I sought to include as much information as possible for any level of salesperson – so veterans should not be offended at some of the basic examples I provide as they will be valuable to someone just starting out in the job. My opinions come from experience and have been tabled with some of the best buyers in North America in order to give the reader some real in-depth knowledge and share what we feel is our retail wisdom.

I do not know of any books of this nature – perhaps since buyers never have a minute of time for anything else as our world, like most other jobs, is a non-stop rollercoaster of blood sweat and tears. I wrote this book in the hours after my family had gone to bed, on planes flying around the world and any other moment I could find downtime. By writing it while in a major buying role it allowed me to analyse specific situations and pass on the learning to you - the salesperson always looking for new ways to close the deal and be the best.

The end result of this project is what I consider a very complete and extremely valuable guide to a buyer's life that will open many doors for a salesperson in any product line – hard goods, fashion, grocery, widgets and trinkets. Absorb it all and use it to your selling advantage.

1

Welcome to My World

I was inspired to write this book one night while reading Steve Schiffman's *The 25 Sales Habits of Highly Effective Salespeople*. Just as you are looking for insight into my world, I was reading up on yours. Schiffman has written several very valuable books directed at sales people and how to sell. There is definitely a lot to learn from these types of books and I'd highly recommend reading them – complimented with this of course – the buyer's perspective.

My world is complicated, stressful and fast-paced. I go through happy moments when sales are great and angry moments when things don't go as planned. I meet a lot of people – some are amazing, efficient, kind and helpful while others are rude, clueless, useless and extremely unhelpful! I get hundreds of emails a day (many from people working out of their garage trying to make it big), tons of phone calls, attend numerous meetings in any given week and have people dropping by my office non-stop looking for answers and other distractions. To say the least – it's not for the faint of heart. Let's not even talk about the economic recession!

Once my annual budget is handed to me I need to come up with a game plan to hit said budget and I need my vendor partners and a bunch of their best products in order to do that – this is where you come in. You want my business and I may or may not want yours. Only so many vendors and products will make it on my shelves, so it becomes quite the rat race for you to break through the buyer's armour. That is what the pages ahead are for – helping you understand my world (and therefore any buyer's world) and that will allow you to play your cards the right way to be one of the "chosen few".

In my world there are several things to understand before you even attempt to contact me. These are likely to apply to all buyers in all categories, as at a basic level we have one job description; buy low, sell lots and make money. Here are some key things to take into consideration when contemplating that initial phone call:

I am insanely busy – all the time!

I hate that I can't kick my feet up on my desk and talk football with my co-workers but from the minute I get in to the office in the morning to the time I leave (and even evenings and weekends unfortunately). I have fifty tasks on my to-do list, get two hundred emails a day, and field about fifty phone calls – half of which are your fellow sales people looking for my business just like you.

Most buyers will start their day checking the previous day's sales and organizing their day. Mondays are perhaps the busiest mornings as a lot of analysis of weekend sales is likely going on, and then that turns to planning the rest of your week - so as my first of many recommendations in the book - consider Monday a write-off. Mid-week late morning to end of day is your best chance to get someone to actually pick up the phone.

The phone is not a terrible way to make an introduction, but a cold call may catch a buyer in the middle of those fifty tasks and their concentration level on your call will be about thirty percent. If you do call, you may want to intentionally make it a short introductory call and ask if there is a good time to call them back, or if you could send some information over email. This is the best way to approach it – trust me – you will either get "no, that's ok I have time now" or they will set a time for a call, a face-to-face meeting or most likely defer you to email.

Email always seems like a brush-off, but it's actually not. If I answered my phone every time it rang, that is all I would do all day. With email, and all the ways now to access it, it's easier for a buyer to manage. All your information is in the email (if I want to read it now or save it for later) and it's easy enough for me to send a quick response. If I have to call you back it becomes task number fifty-one on the list, but if I can just type a quick one-liner on email - we are rolling along. I can do that on my phone in a cab in China if I need to.

We all have our calendars on our computers and most of the time they are part of our email system (eg: Microsoft Outlook) so email makes it easy to schedule a meeting or call right then and there.

Which brings me to another very important lesson; DON'T BE A STALKER! Seriously, if there is one thing that takes you out of a buyer's *favourite sales person* list its non-stop calls and multiple random emails. I get if we are working on a big deal or project and we need to swap information back and forth to get it done – totally acceptable. But if you call me repeatedly to say hello and ask me how much your product sold yesterday, or in the last hour since you last called me – I will a) ask you to cool your jets, b) not respond to you or c) call your boss (if you were warned and continued the behaviour) to let them know there is a vein bulging out of my head and it has your name on it.

"One wish I had for a salesperson was that they understood their product was not the only product I managed," stated a former Senior Buyer at Target. "I managed sixteen racks of product, plus had financial and marketing responsibility for my area. Most days, I was stuck in meetings from 8-5 and could only do my job before or after that. It could take me up to several days to get back to them. Sending me more messages or calling me incessantly wasn't going to change that. I had to prioritize or never leave work. If it wasn't my biggest priority, I wasn't going to answer no matter how much they called or how many emails were sent. Those sales people who helped me prioritize were the ones that were most effective in getting me to work with them."

Again, a buyer is very busy – especially the more product count, volume or store count they have. Get on their good side by not being a time-eater. Your more strategic approach to contacting the buyer will pay off in the end.

I have a game plan already – how do you fit into it?

If you know the buying cycles of a particular commodity or category then use this to your advantage in making that first contact. What I mean by this is: call me when my assortment plan is a blank slate. By doing this I take into consideration new products or vendors because my goal is to have the optimal assortment. Typically this is a seasonal refresh in most businesses – in the New Year as a new fiscal calendar starts or if my business is for example Christmas Décor I might be looking to finalize my plan by June.

It is very hard to get in with similar products to what I already have stock of in my stores – my plans are baked with existing partners and there are promises to keep. What you can do (and this is very important at any time) is make a list of my assortment today – products, prices, shelf position, brand mix – and look for GAPS. A gap is just that – a hole in the assortment that customers need. For example - if I buy disposable tableware and you see that I have a five, ten and twenty-five pack paper plates, a five and ten pack cups and every configuration of plastic utensils known to man, then you know:

- You only have one play on the utensils – winning on cost
- You also know cost may be the only play on plates, unless you can show me statistics that point to a great need for fifty pack plates for people who feel the need to invite everyone they have ever known to their kid's birthday party. In this case you better have a really great cost on the fifty pack that makes it a no-brainer for me to want my customer to buy fifty. In the current assortment I would be hoping they buy the twenty-five pack and make a return trip before party time if they need more, or buy two twenty-five packs
- So your easiest gap to focus on would be a twenty-five pack of cups because I sell that in plates and can provide that in utensils - but not in cups.

Knowing my assortment and where you can fill a hole is just smart selling. I don't need another product similar to what I already have, I don't need another vendor to deal with (please refer to the last section on me having very little time), and I if I did replace one brand with your product I would need to exit the old product, give up any back end funding associated with it, change the product out on my counter and several other steps that I would only do if it was truly worth it to do. But if you can convince me that your product is an enhancement to my assortment and will ADD and not simply just REPLACE profit for me I am all ears.

If you do your homework and you know that I'm doing an assortment overhaul in the future then you can wisely pitch me in plenty of time to get visions of your product and the value of your brand inside my head. There are a few ways to figure out when the best time is:

- Industry trade shows are always timed with typical product lifecycles – for example the New York Toy Fair is held in January each year because buyers need to make decisions on their holiday toy line-up by Spring at the latest since these toys then need to be forecasted and ordered four to five months in advance to allow for production time if they are to land in Fall
- Major manufacturers often have a similar product launch schedule each year – often early in the New Year and perhaps a second in Fall for holiday. Major retailers can sometimes have a say in when these products release, but most likely time their resets around the manufacturer's launch dates. If you know these dates use them to your advantage.
- Do an exploratory call to the buyer or their assistant asking when the best time to pitch them product is. If you keep the call or email quick and painless most buyers will let you know and may even enquire about what you have – but don't scare them off – think long-term and call during holiday for next year business.
- If you know fellow salesmen that already deal with the buyer then you could see if they are willing to play nice and share the information.

December in many categories is a good time to get a foot in the door. December may be the thick of the holiday period (and definitely an extremely busy time for buyers trying to capitalize on the largest selling month of the year) but it is also when, based on new product lifecycles, buyers need to start planning for the upcoming year. This is a great time to get their attention and set up a meeting that month or in January (when most retailers get a breather). When you get in early your name gets tossed in the hat when the buyer is going through their mental list of vendor possibilities for the upcoming year.

I am Prepared To See You...Are You Prepared To See Me?

I know you want to see me, because you want to sell me loads of various stuff and make a bunch of money — but are you rushing it? I love meeting new people, I love growing my business and shooting for the stars, I love to discover new exciting products, but if you are not ready to present me anything meaningful yet - I don't need to see you.

If you have an idea for a product you think I will drool profusely over, think again about setting up a meeting for me to see your smiling face and talk about a phantom product that you draw in stick-figure form on the whiteboard of my meeting room. I can't sell ideas to my customers — and, as we reviewed already, I don't have the time to. If you are presenting that idea in a forum that I can weigh in on when I can find the time, then that may be different (such as a trade show booth or an online idea site). You may send an email out to get some opinions but don't be too disheartened if you do not see any responses back on it. Ideas are for product creation experts and they will have the retail intelligence to know if it's worthwhile building and putting money into — and whether it is worthy enough to present to buyers.

"I preferred first to be emailed the product with an explanation and then called as a follow up," explained a former Senior Buyer at Target. "I need time to absorb before the conversation."

11

"I think it is best for a new vendor to do the research to figure out the appropriate channels to get their foot in the door, and follow them," says a Senior Buyer at Old Navy. "Most companies should have that information available to outside vendors. I don't feel it is a best foot forward when they contact you via personal networking sites or name drop."

If you are just starting out you have to make sure you are in a position to deal with a retailer. I have had people set a meeting with me (even though I was reluctant to do so) and then pitch me like I had two dollar stores and not like I was a multi-billion dollar international retailer. I will share the details of this meeting for those of you new to the sales world so you can look to avoid making the same errors. In the meeting the salesman made the following mistakes:

- He brought one sample that was not in retail packaging and did not yet know what his packaging plan would be if he landed a business larger than his own personal website

- He presented a volume discount plan (eg: buy 1-10 units for 10.00 each, buy 11-20 for 8.00 each etc) – which maybe some outlets are used to but not major retailers. He was already deep into looking about as small-time as he could at that point but this really drove it home. Just give me the cost of the product and we can work out what discounts or adjustments I would need

- He was extremely nervous and this created disorganization (fumbling through papers, scrambled dialog). We have all been there so I can't be too hard on him but you need to be prepared to take on the stress of a meeting like that

- He did not have distribution set up so if I actually did want to buy his product with its yet-to-be-designed packaging, I would have to wait until he figured out how he was going to get it to me – because he knew his eight year old's red wagon would not be accepted at the doors of my distribution center. This isn't so bad, but how can I be quoted a cost if you don't know how much your shipping and distribution costs are going to be? You should at least have a ballpark cost you have researched and incorporate it into the cost of the product - then scramble to find a distributor that fits that price – or else you would have to come back to me later and say "oh sorry, I need to raise your cost to twelve dollars from ten because I didn't factor in logistics"
- He didn't know if I carried anything similar...come on – go to one of my stores or at least the retailer's website and take a look around. It could be embarrassing if I carried the same product already (as many times I see the identical product pitched to me by a few people because there are only so many factories in Asia making these products and crafty entrepreneurs will "buy off the shelf" as we call it, and slap their logo on it and shop it around to retailers) and worse - its half the price you are quoting me
- He only had one lone sample. Now this is fine if it's a prototype and was meant just as an example, but in this case this was a finished product. I don't know about other buyers but with certain products I won't buy before I try – I refuse to give my customers a bad experience (as that can be very damaging to my store's reputation) so I am going to test my products and make

13

sure they work properly first. If you are going to go for the big fish then spend the extra one hundred bucks on some extra samples so it can be tested, as you again look very small-time saying "I can't give you one to try – I only have one". If it's a cheap product and you do give out a sample and we do business, or could potentially at some point, my advice is to also avoid asking for it back later on – samples are a part of the business and asking for a five dollar sample after a month would scare off any buyer (unless you work for a company, and there are some out there, that forces you to manage your samples and may even dock your pay if they are not returned. In this case let the buyer know so at least they understand the circumstances)

I know this all sounds a bit tough on the poor fellow - we did have a friendly chat over coffee and parted ways (perhaps I helped him gain insight and confidence for future selling attempts), but this is business and you may only get one shot at the grand prize – this was NOT a best foot forward for him or his product, and it now serves as a learning for others through this book.

The rest of the book will help you to cover your bases one hundred and ten percent, but from the examples above you can clearly see that you have to know exactly the right timing to come in and pitch your goods. You need to be sure you know what I'm looking for and be ready to pitch it so that I want to sign you up on the spot.

Three Keys to Selling

You have to approach the prospect of selling your product with confidence, planning and research. The confidence part is just as important as the other two – be sure of yourself and your product's value to me as a buyer. To get me excited about a new product requires you to make your own excitement contagious. Go into the battle expecting to succeed because I can tell when a salesperson doesn't believe in the product they are pitching and it often makes me second guess picking that product up.

Planning is what this book will help you with the most. In general though, you need to map out how you are going to approach selling me a product from beginning to the end – getting a meeting, handling the meeting, what samples to show, what is the marketing plan, how are you going to get me the product to sell and so on. There are so many different aspects (as you will soon learn) and often a short window of opportunity – so ensure you are prepared.

Research is part of the planning process, but I highlight it separately because it can be the difference between winning and losing. Doing your homework and know where your product fits into my plans, how my stores work, what competitors of yours and mine are doing, how the market advertises, what I want from a partner and other important aspects of the business – these are the pieces of the puzzle that you can use to be the best at what you do. Your in-depth knowledge of these aspects of the business make me and your peers think "wow, this person is amazing – they are really on top of things" – and from there you gain trust, respect and a lot more of the word "yes" in our conversations!

If you feel that you have accomplished the points detailed in this chapter it is a good idea to take inventory of what you have in place. Make a checklist of key areas that need to be prepared before our first meeting. Some points to include from this chapter are:

- Initial introductory email to touch base with buyer
- Visit buyer's stores to see what products I am up against
- Visit buyer's competitors to see what I'm up against there too
- Chart out where my products fall in line with what they have
- Highlight the gaps in the assortment I can help fill
- I have checked that this is a good time to introduce new products (buying cycle)
- I have a product, samples and distribution and pricing lined up already
- I know how to speak to a retail buyer on their terms
- I have practiced my pitch repeatedly and feel I am ready

If you can check off this list and add a few other lines specific to your pitch, you should be ready to set up our first meeting. If it is your first time approaching a retail buyer then see if you can find someone with experience to give you some tips. If not, no problem – the rest of the book will guide you whether you are brand spanking new or a crafty veteran of the selling game. Now go make that meeting set-up call with confidence!

"I lose respect for any vendor who calls me and says, "I have a product that you need." When I further query them, I determine that the guy has never been in one of my stores! That drives me crazy!" – A Buyer at Dollar General

2

Our Meetings

Now that you have a meeting lined up – either in person or over the phone – you obviously want to capitalize on this opportunity! Most meetings are going to be half an hour or an hour, which is not a lot of time, so you need to go in with a game plan and buyers across the globe beg of you to stick to your allotted time.

Sometimes we encounter overzealous salespeople who can't get their message across in the given meeting time and proceed to ignore the fact that the meeting is over. People who go over their time disrespect both my time and that of the next person I am supposed to be meeting with (or your next meeting). There are some times where I may be free to keep talking and want to keep the dialog going – the best thing to do is manage your time and acknowledge the end of the meeting and then ask if there is time left to finish up discussions. That gives the buyer the option to say yes or no as opposed to feeling rude by cutting the meeting off (yes, some buyers do have a heart). Again, the best thing is to be well planned enough to get everything in during the meeting timeframe.

What does a well-planned meeting look like? Everyone is different, but I like to get the introductions and small talk out of the way early – the more detailed 'get to know ya' stuff comes once you've established some business and are having a relaxing lunch or dinner or higher level meeting. These are your goals:

- Introductions
- About your company and overview of products (history, flagship products, distribution channels, factory information, annual revenue etc)
- Show you have done your homework – YOU tell ME what gaps I have and how you are going to fill them
- Go over your products
- Explain the advantages of your product over others
- Ask me what I think and what I am looking for in a brand
- Think on your feet – use whatever I just said I was looking for to your advantage and tell me you can do that or at least look into how your company can suit my needs
- Keep to your time and wrap up
- Review the meeting and come up with next steps
- Don't float – shake my hand and go

I cannot stress enough how important doing your homework is here. You can really derail things if you are all over the board in meetings – if I need another twenty pack of paper plates like I need a hole in the head and you spend forty-five of sixty minutes telling me that the twenty pack is where the business is at and how wonderful it is, then you have fifteen minutes to rescue the Titanic. Know what your goals and my goals are together and be precise and to-the-point. Tell me what gaps you see and how you just happen to have the best one of those in the market with massive quantities and a hot price. Make me drool over the car I'm going to buy with the gigantic bonus I am going to get from selling so many of them!

There are several things to watch for in your conversations with me that are helpful to know so you don't end up in an uncomfortable position or awkward conversation. These are common things salespeople say that could have detrimental consequences:

"This product is selling really well at [insert retailer name here]" – It is not a terrible statement, but be sure you can back that up...too often salespeople use this type of line to embellish a product's potential with me and I WILL call you on it; "really – what does 'well' mean? Is it outselling their top products? Is it headed for top spot in market share?" – If it's not blowing the doors off then it's a weak statement to make so remove it from your repertoire!

"Ooooh, look at that – don't you just love how that looks!" – This is a statement used in the vendor buddy system – where one person in the meeting (typically the product manager) shows me a new product and their partner (usually the salesperson) tries to make a new stapler model seem like a Ferrari was just pulled out of the box. This is another weak tactic that none of us buy into, and frankly it makes most of us uncomfortable. You should avoid attempts to steer my reaction to a product with this type of tactic – trust me, I will tell you what I really think of it.

"[Your number one competitor] really liked this item" – 'hearsay' I believe is the lawyer term for this – how would I ever know that this is actually true? By saying it I am not sure if you mean that they are interested and therefore you are bullying me a bit to get me to buy it, or maybe you are just saying the general opinion of similar retailers is that it is a good item – which is fine, but what's to say I even want to look at something my competitor likes. You are also telling me by saying it that you showed the new product to my rival before you showed it to me…which a buyer may take offense to. I don't expect you to show me every product first (although some buyers may - so remember that) but you don't have to tell me I was two, three or four on your list. These are my mortal enemies in the retail world – I may not care what they think.

"You probably don't know about this new technology…" – You want to avoid statements that imply that the buyer is not educated on the category. Assume they may know or ask them "are you familiar with this new technology?"

"I have a bomb strapped to my chest and I'll blow us all to pieces if you don't buy my stuff" – I am just making sure you are still paying attention! In case you were wondering, this is a BAD statement as well.

These are professional people you are dealing with. Your job after the first handshake is to get to know them well and make friends with them. Once you know them you can decide what they may want to hear and how they should be handled.

Another situation to be careful of that occurs often is when a salesperson works top-down in a meeting. They sit in a room with the buyer, the buyer's boss, and the VP for example and they make every pitch, show every sample and make all eye contact with the VP. Yes, he is the highest ranking official in the room but guess what…he most likely has absolutely NOTHING to do with the sku decisions. This should fall under the buyer's job description and is what the buyer gets paid to do. You may be trying to impress the company leaders, but if it was the buyer you came to see and who arranged for you to come in and present – don't treat them like a vagrant who just walked in from the street – they will ultimately decide what business you do, so you should direct your presentation at them as well and to each audience member equally. Trust me – the VP won't be offended you didn't focus on them...but the buyer will be.

"I find it awkward when there is a lot of silence in a meeting," noted a former Buyer for Best Buy. "Either something has gone wrong or the vendor did not have a game plan going in on who would speak – or they didn't brush up on what they are presenting."

One of the things that make salespeople look like they have not learned about their products is reading off a spec sheet while presenting a product. Now, when I say this I should stress that it is ok, to a point, to cheat a bit and glance at a presentation the product manager gave you to assist in presenting the product – but if you came to hype me up on the greatest product since sliced bread and you have taped the five bullet points about the product on the back of the sample you are holding up for me to see, I have lost all respect for you right then and there. This is unacceptable – you need to take half an hour the night before our meeting and read up on the key points and be polished enough to at least present those. I in no way expect you to be able to assemble a TV set in front of me and describe each component, but if you can't remember that it is a forty-two inch LCD flat panel with 1080P and internet ready...you should think about finding an alternate career. Besides, you sell this stuff for a living – show some enthusiasm about it.

I am obviously going to ask you at least a few questions – some you may not know and have to look up or tell me "I am not sure, I will find out and email you when I get back to the office," but I shouldn't surprise you with a basic question – even on a brand new product that just landed in your hands the day

21

before. There is no shame in deferring to an expert on the product that's with you or reporting back later. Whatever you do – DON'T GUESS. Better to get back to someone than look bad by guessing wrong.

If you have an expert with you then arrange with them ahead of time to rescue you in case you get stuck. Some teams are great at this – they will go back and forth in the meeting filling in gaps that one another may have in their explanation, but ensure you are not giving the buyer whiplash from the conversation – the salesperson takes the lead if that is the plan of attack and the support people interject as needed and keep it short and sweet. If the supporting staff take over the meeting it really comes across like the salesperson is inefficient and not needed, and you don't want that thinking going on obviously. Take back your meeting if that happens to you – tactfully of course, as to not offend your boss or product manager, but don't let it keep going and derail your presentation while you sink into your chair and become background scenery.

If you are going to show samples of product to me – make sure they are professional – don't come to the meeting with a coffee maker sample that has cracked glass on the carafe and the on-off switch falls off when you press it. You can always say "it's just a prototype" (which is great because it means I am seeing the product before it even goes into production) but it still needs to have some quality to it. A flimsy sample doesn't give me much confidence that the real thing is going to be any better – despite you telling me twenty times during our meeting that it will. You may want to go with artists renderings (drawings of the product concept at the early stages) instead of a terrible handmade sample held together by tape and staples. If you do show a rendering or prototype, make sure to send the real thing when it's ready so the buyer knows it ended up like it was described.

If you are still in the prototype phase of product development be sure to ask for the buyer's feedback on it if you trust their opinion – often a long-time buyer will see things even your engineers may have overlooked because they a) have been dealing with products for years and b) they have seen many products from other manufacturers and may tip you off to a cool feature that they may have seen from your competitors. Including the buyer in product development, even if they don't add a lot of value to the conversations, is a great gesture – it shows a high level of partnership and that you don't have a "you need to just buy whatever we put in front of you" attitude. Put it this way: if the buyer feels they were a part of the process and had a hand in making a product in any way they will definitely give that product special attention when it hits the stores!

Speaking

To me, the number one trait of a great leader is the ability to speak well to others. Look at business leaders like Steve Jobs – people who can convince anyone to do anything with the power of their words and how they present them. A good salesperson is no different – Steve Jobs is selling the general public on an idea or product, while you are selling me on carrying your merchandise. You need to take command of the meeting and show your passion for the product (no matter what you are selling) and that passion should rub off on me and my team and make us want your products in our stores immediately. A great salesperson, through the ability to speak effectively, can sell a line of staplers like they were Jobs pitching the iPhone to the mass public for the first time. It can be your most deadly selling weapon.

"A good Powerpoint presentation really lands it for me," explained a Buyer for Best Buy. "If I see they made an effort to put together a nice, professional presentation then it elevates that salesperson's status versus someone who clearly whipped something together last minute and didn't care enough about what they were pitching. A half-effort presentation makes me think that's how they run the rest of their business. I understand if there are circumstances behind having to rush a presentation – that happens, but if that is the norm then it just isn't professional."

When you are in a meeting presenting an idea or the benefits of a product you are in the spotlight. If you don't like the focus on you then you may just want to find a new profession. Since you are already down this job road you will need to take advantage of your time in that spotlight. With all eyes on you – what will you do at that very moment to secure the business or gain more of it? Would you fumble through papers, leave periods of long silence, say "ummm" fifty times and read from a computer screen without eye contact with those you are trying to impress? You would be shocked at how often that occurs in this business. Don't be that person.

If you are not a strong speaker there are several avenues you can go down to improve:

- Toastmasters is a public speaking group with one or more clubs in most cities across North America – it is a great learning experience for any level of professional and has best-in-class training materials

- There may be weekend courses you can take locally that teach you speech techniques that may be very helpful. These may also tie into presentation skills and perhaps even improving your Powerpoint skills to go along with your speaking

- Find a mentor who you consider a strong speaker or presenter – pick their brain on how they elevated their game, how they developed themselves into a powerful speaker and just being around them and absorbing their style will help greatly. If they have a certain way of getting a point across don't be afraid to steal the technique and build on it. For example, if they pound their fist on the desk every time they want to drive home a critical point and YOU take notice every time – then likely this will work in some situations you may be in and you should try it out and see if it helps

The good ole standing in front of the mirror and saying your pitch over and over technique actually works – if you get nervous before speaking in front of people, be it two or two hundred, you will find that the more you know the speech and are able to practice it enough to say it with minimal notes or none at all, the easier it will be to deliver. It's all about confidence – if you know all there is to know about the topic you can tell everyone about it as if you were explaining it to your spouse over a glass of wine in the kitchen. Most fear in public speaking comes from a lack of confidence – the fear of looking like a fool, stumbling on words, saying the wrong thing or people judging you. Forget that stuff and make sure you know it inside and out and just go out and talk about it with ease.

Travelling To Meet

Travelling can be an enjoyable part of the job for a buyer and a salesperson – a break from the everyday routine, a chance to let loose and get to know business partners and co-workers and is also a chance to see new cities and attractions. Use these trips for those purposes and strengthen your relationship with the buyer.

Business trips can be very tiring and hectic and many buyers are reluctant to sign up for them as there is always too much going on at the office to take time away (it's hard enough to take time off for holidays let alone be away from the office with limited access to email and resources for a few days or a week). Knowing that position for the buyer, make sure your planned trip is valuable to all attending. If it is something you can accomplish by dropping by the office then just do that. If it is a chance for the buyer and perhaps their bosses to meet your upper management, talk face to face with product designers, have a hand in product development, land major long-term partnerships and plans and learn more about your company and its people – it's a beautiful thing.

These trips are very valuable and depending on the size of the relationship they should be done. If you and I are planning to do fifty thousand dollars of business next year I wouldn't bank on either of our bosses to approve us spending a couple thousand dollars on a trip to your office in downtown New York. If we are going to bake a ten million dollar plan then two grand is a laughable amount of expenditure to invest in our relationship.

Those trips need to be productive, but not a health risk for the buyer. If I am coming from the West Coast to the East Coast there is a three hour time difference. This means that although you want to get every minute out of your two thousand dollar investment, scheduling a meeting at eight in the morning means I am starting the meeting at five o'clock and waking up to get ready at four o'clock. This makes me very grumpy and causes me to a) note your inconsiderate scheduling and b) be less attentive to your meeting because I am sleeping with my eyes open. I get WHY you do it, but it's not a great gesture so I'd cautions against it.

Some buyers love the pampering and attention given to them by their vendors and you just need to know who you are dealing with to know how to manage the trip. Know what they are all about before you try pouring vodka down their throat at a strip club in the shadiest part of town. If you don't know them well, ask the right questions to make your decision:

- What do you feel like eating for dinner?

- Have you been to [the city you're in] before?

- Are there any places you wanted to go while you are here?

- What do you do for fun back home?

- Are you into sports? There's a great sports bar downtown...

The more you ask the more you can get a sense of what they are all about – you should be doing this anyway to get to know them, but ease into the wild outings. Some retailers, such as Walmart, have strict policies around travel, dinners and other situations that may be perceived as "advantageous" to the buyer-vendor relationship.

Be On Time!

I should not even have to say this but...do NOT be late for our meetings. Nothing (except punching me in the face during a meeting) tells me you have no respect for my time than being casually late. I say "casually" because sometimes people are just late – traffic, eating a bad burrito for lunch...it happens. But if you just roll in when you feel like it and assume I'm just sitting around with nothing to do so I can be flexible – you are wrong. I personally like to stack all my meetings into one or two 'meeting days' each week, so I am in back to back to back meetings on those days. If you are ten minutes late you throw my whole schedule off or simply get that much less time – which hurts both of us.

If you are going to be late then call or email me and let me know as soon as you know in order to cover yourself. If you don't have a good reason – make one up (as long as it's believable of course). If you have half an hour booked and you will be fifteen minutes late then perhaps asking to reschedule is a better idea. You should always plan on leaving extra early to cover random delays like a ten-car pile-up on the road to my office or Godzilla standing outside your door when you go to get into your car. Why take the chance? Have everything you need prepared ahead of time and pre-packed ready to go. If you have meetings before ours ensure you leave the meeting before on time and allow more than enough travel time between meetings. It is NOT ok that you are late for our meeting because you ran over with another buyer from my company – you are still disrespecting my time.

Get Off Your Phone!

There are a lot of pet peeves of mine that have been very therapeutic for me to get off my chest and into this book to help salespeople in their quest for the optimal vendor-buyer relationship - so thank you. One in particular I cannot stress enough: do NOT leave your ringer on during our meeting. Unless your wife is going into labor or someone is seriously hurt, there are not too many situations that warrant you picking up your phone in the middle of our meeting and starting to have a conversation. If you picture the scenario in your head – us carrying on a conversation and your phone ringing and interrupting us, then you picking it up and starting to talk...does that not sound like a very disrespectful situation? Yes it is. Then why does it happen with some salespeople?

Some people may be expecting an important call, which is fine. Let me know ahead of time that this may happen and that you apologize in advance. We have all been in that situation and it's not an issue, but pre-warning me stops me from being shocked that you answered your phone. If you do need to answer it try to keep the conversation short if you can – you are eating up our meeting time. Another suggestion is to set the ringer to vibrate as it is less aggravating for the person you are with. If there are other people from your team in the meeting and they can carry on the meeting be sure to excuse yourself and take the call in the hallway or another room.

Texting or messaging of any kind throughout our meeting is also unacceptable. Too often you find a person in a larger meeting preoccupied messaging with people on their phone. Nothing says "you have lost my interest" or "I have better things to do and I'm not paying attention" than looking down under the table at your phone or worse – doing it in plain sight. You may as well be sleeping through the meeting! Some people are just so attached to their smart phones that they can't help themselves – we all know one of "those" people, but it is a terrible habit and extremely rude so don't be that person.

Senior Management Involvement in Meetings

Our bosses are typically called upon to help build relationships with other companies and if we do enough volume together or want to explore doing more business they may end up in our meetings. There is no issue with this at all – it's a great thing most of the time to have the ear of the higher-ups. If you have brought them in to help complain about the buyer it may not be so pleasant and you will want to judge whether that is a good move or if it will burn bridges with your buyer. If it is to help grow the relationship here are a few tips to making sure this now higher-level meeting works in your favor:

- Make sure the buyer is aware of who is coming in and what level they are at – and if they expect someone above them to also attend

- Fill your boss in on what is going on in your business before the meeting – the last thing you or the buyer needs is your boss asking questions you answered two months earlier or battling on long-since-resolved issues and eating up all that valuable meeting time

- Let the buyer know what to expect from your boss – this ensures they feel comfortable and not taken by surprise by their personality or tactics

- In some situations where you and the buyer agree that you both want to ensure your bosses see you have a handle on the business, you can collaborate on a meeting game plan — what to say and what not to, the direction of the meeting and how you will lead the conversation

- Never blame. Throwing the buyer under the bus in front of their boss is rough and obviously the buyer will be angry with you for it. If you get challenged by something try to find ways to downplay the situation or answer in a less critical way that doesn't pierce the heart of the buyer sitting across from you (unless that was your intention of course). If the buyer was not at fault then you should avoid making them look bad to cover up something you did wrong obviously — that never ends up working out well

You will want to let each other know of any topics that may come up so nobody looks like a fool on either side. If you have not told me you are raising the cost by ten percent on every sku in the assortment and your boss throws it out in the meeting thinking it's been covered already it will be a big shock to the buyer and make you look bad in front of both of them for not having brought up such an important nugget of information prior. Your boss doesn't always get to see you in action — this is where they judge you and your sales skills - so make sure it all runs smoothly.

Arguing with your partners

If you are presenting to me alongside some other people from your company you should remember that, although we are all friends here, I don't need to see you unravel in front of me and

31

fight with each other. You would be surprised how often this happens. It may be just a small incident like one person making a statement and the other rolling their eyes or someone correcting another in a harsh tone, but even these little outbursts look unprofessional and make me wonder if your company has their house in order. Decide ahead of time who pitches what and make sure you are in agreement on what you are saying. Trust me – a well-oiled machine is very impactful where everyone presenting is clicking with each other and the opposite is true when it's a free-for-all.

Write it Down

When we are in a meeting I highly suggest you take notes. Even if you don't write anything down, at least have something available in case we make plans of some kind and you for some reason want to actually remember them. I know some people have incredible memories, but I still don't trust that anyone is going to remember everything – and you don't want to have to ask again later what it was we agreed upon. If I say I want one thousand pieces of your product during our meeting and you don't write it down, I'm most likely thinking to myself that you are not going to action my request.

One of the things I love about my best vendors is when they take plenty of notes in our meetings and then send the recap on email within a few days. This shows they are eager and engaged and it also really helps me out - as I like to have a record of everything myself. I would suggest using a tablet or notebook computer to take notes as hand-writing notes means you are going to have to double your work by retyping the notes into your computer. I use an excel spreadsheet with each of my vendor's having a separate tab and I keep a running list of notes by vendor by date. It allows me to reference back to all our conversations in one central place. When I used to take notes on a pad of paper I'd have to flip through fifty pages of scribbled notes to find what I was looking for – using a spreadsheet saved me time and my sanity!

"Sometimes a vendor gets the day or week wrong – even when THEY are the ones that sent the Outlook invite that we both have in our calendars," laughed a former Buyer for Best Buy. "I sit there waiting for reception to let me know they are here but nobody ever shows up. I angrily call the vendor and they say "that's next week isn't it?" It makes me wonder about them. The other one is vendors from another time zone who don't reset their watches when they come for meetings. If they are from another city that is an hour behind and they go by what their Outlook calendar said before they left or they are looking at their watch they haven't adjusted and show up an hour late."

Our meetings are where it all happens – make sure you are prepared, polished and respectful. Our first meeting sets the tone for the rest of our relationship and is the key to doing a lot of business, a little bit or none at all. Treat every meeting like the first and learn from each one – get to know what the buyer likes and dislikes, what they want to see and how they want things presented...observe and take notes for future reference. Once you are on the buyer's good side and have a strong working relationship things get much easier and the buyer is much more willing to take meetings with you. If you annoy them they will avoid you like the plague.

"A great vendor is truly a PARTNER in the business and actually cares, watches, reports on, and delivers solutions to the business." – A Fashion Category Manager at Walmart

3

Money Talks

I get paid to do one thing and one thing only – make money for my employer. There are two different kinds of money I get from selling products: top line and bottom line dollars. Top line is definitely important – those are the actual sales dollars that my stores pry from our customer's hands. I do have a top line budget to hit of course and I definitely aim to do that when I plan my business.

More important are bottom line dollars or "profit dollars" that show up after all is said and done and the accountants do their magic calculations. When my P&L (Profit and Loss Statement) is finalized after each month, quarter and year finishes and the numbers come out to the big kahunas in their corner offices they are only focussed on how much money the company actually made.

This number is not simple to arrive at. It starts with sales (we will get to how to help grow those in upcoming chapters) and the budget I was given to achieve at the start of the year. Say I'm in the cookie buying role at a big supermarket chain and my budget for September is six million dollars. To get to my bottom line (the first line of the P&L is the sales line hence the term "top line" and the final profit is the last, hence "bottom line") I need to be sure to hit several financial targets – all having a budget to hit. Some of these include:

- Gross Margin rate
- Shrinkage
- Markdowns
- Marketing costs
- Freight
- Funding
- Foreign exchange
- Inventory costs

Here is how each key line affects my ability to achieve my bottom line:

Besides sales, the other major contributor is gross margin rate (or "mark-up"). This is the difference between the cost I paid for an item from the manufacturer and what retail I sell it for. Different retailers calculate gross margin in a few different ways, but one standard is (retail – cost)/retail. So the math on a ten dollar item at retail that was bought for seven dollars from the vendor would be:

(10-7)/10 = 30% gross margin rate (GM%)

If I sell it on sale for 9.00 then the math becomes:

(9-7)/9 = 22% gross margin rate

So my budget in sales is six million in tasty cookie sales in September and the industry standard is thirty percent gross margin rate. My company felt at budget time that I could get better costs than the market standard and get thirty-two percent gross margin rate. That would make my profit target the following:

$6,000,000 top line sales

32% GM rate

$1,920,000 profit (top line sales x 32% rate)

So now I need to make close to two million dollars from sugar-loving cookie monsters across the country. I negotiate with the vendor for an extra twenty cents on my 7.00 cost cookies I sell for ten dollars and my 6.80 cost gets me my desired 32% gross margin rate.

All of this you probably already knew, but it's great to have a refresher – because your chances of closing the deal with me are exponentially higher when you are looking at the math I'm up against and helping me find ways to exceed my targets!

First of all, you need to understand what my margin targets are. There are few brands powerful enough that I need to carry them and make under my margin target selling them – and I most likely sell them already because I have to – customers demand them. So if you are trying to sell to me and you aren't in the "must have under any circumstance" category, you may not get too far trying to sell me product at twenty-five percent gross margin – seven percent under my GM rate budget. So now that that is understood – here is what you need to do: find a way to EXCEED my margin requirements.

Why, you ask, should you give me more margin? Because I need to offset the big bad national brand giving me low margin and forcing me to live with it. You can swoop in and be my knight in shining cookie armour...save me from missing my margin target. Here is the scenario if I sell half of my September sales budget with the lower-margin national brand:

$3,000,000 national brand sales at 25% margin = $750,000 profit

This means I can't just sell the rest of my $3,000,000 (the other half of my $6,000,000 budget) at my 32% margin. I am too far away making seven percent UNDER my margin target on the national brand. I need to make up the shortfall with the remaining three million in business:

$6,000,000 of sales at 32% gross margin = $1,920,000 (my budget)

$1,920,000 minus $750,000 (what I already made with the national brand) = $1,170,000 of profit left to make on the remaining $3,000,000 of sales I will need to do

That means I need to sell the remaining products at 39% margin ($1,170,000 divided into $3,000,000). So I need your brand of delicious non-national branded cookies to deliver thirty-nine to forty percent margin to make my profit budget.

If the industry standard is thirty percent margin then you can bet there are not a lot of brands willing to offer me upwards of forty percent. But believe me – if you have cookies acceptable for human consumption that will sell and I can offset the lower margin national brand with your higher-margin product then we just might have a good thing going.

Now you know the way to my heart. But there are other P&L lines that you can also win me over by understanding my challenges with.

Shrinkage

A big challenge is "shrinkage" or loss from things like theft or other situations where money is lost unknowingly. If you are selling me cosmetics (a high-shrink category) for example then you may want to work into your plans a display fixture that somehow cuts down on theft or offer me a "shrink allowance" on top of my margin percent that kicks back some dollars to my bottom line to cover some of the inevitable losses I will face. Many companies do not acknowledge shrink and leave that up to the retailer to deal with – here is your chance to win the business by showing you recognize it is an issue and doing something over and above to fight it.

I can make my sales and margin and be cruising toward hitting budget for the month, but have a big loss from a wave of cookie thefts and miss my P&L by thousands.

Markdowns

Markdowns can be challenging in any category. What happens at the end of a product's lifecycle? Say I am the buyer for computer software – a category where new updated programs are always coming out. I have a tax software for 2011 and that tax year is now done. At this point the 2011 version is useless to everyone and I couldn't sell it if my life depended on it.

I have three different paths I can take:

- One where I buy very conservatively because I don't want to have a bunch left over that I will need to lose money writing off (or "marking down" and having that hit my markdown line on my P&L)

- One where I buy more aggressively, run the risk of not selling them all and run into costly markdowns
- One where I negotiate write-off dollars from you or a return of any unsold units by a pre-determined timeframe (eg: one week after taxes are due to be filed).

With the first scenario of buying conservatively I may buy ten thousand units on a potential demand of fifteen thousand, whereas if I knew I was covered for anything I over-bought I would buy all fifteen thousand. You would get the extra five thousand in sales as opposed to those five thousand sitting in your warehouse and you potentially would not have to shell out a dime to me if I sold them all. In the tax software scenario it only makes sense – you would have needed to write them off regardless, so you may as well try to sell them in my stores.

You would obviously need to plan out a dollar reserve for the worst-case scenario happening. Although the write-off or return play (known as a "guaranteed sale") is always the best motivator for a buyer (eliminate the risk!), the smart play is to monitor sales closely through the selling period before the agreed upon end date. This is where forecasting the sales velocity on a daily or weekly basis is essential. Say I buy ten thousand units for a ten week window of sales before I get to return the left-overs back to you. My average weekly sales (assuming no major sales spikes are planned) are estimated (forecasted) at one thousand a week. You would need to monitor for the following scenario:

The first two weeks I sell 800 each week and not the 2000 during that period I anticipated

I am already 200 a week short - so 400 under forecast in the first two weeks

I now have to sell 8400 instead of 8000 in the remaining eight weeks – and I'm not on a good pace! I am on pace to under-sell by 2000 units that you would need to write off in the end

Let's say each unit is worth 5.00 – you are looking at a tough $10,000 cheque you will need to write to me if I have 2000 left

The best thing to do here is something that, in my many years of experience, many vendors just never seem to grasp: give me 2.00 a unit in a sell-through for one week to discount the product. We all know that nine times out of ten a product sells more when discounted. If I could sell 2800 units in week seven on sale with me not losing any margin rate because you gave me the 2.00 to lower my cost that week, then I just made up the 2000 units I was on pace to be short sales on. Assuming I go back to selling 800 in weeks eight to ten at full price - I sell everything and you do not have as big a cheque to write. Your sell-through cost you $5,600 (2800 units x 2.00) as opposed to the $10,000.

Me losing money on a vendor's product always hurts, and makes me cautious the next time I buy from them or I look for someone else with less risk.

Inventory Costs

Lines such as inventory costs are also important. There are costs associated with holding inventory and this is another good thing for you to understand in our relationship. In a nutshell, every retailer is financed for their inventory. That inventory financing is not free – there is interest associated with it, so the name of the game is what retailers call "turnover" or "turns" – how fast a product sells through in a given timeframe.

If I buy three thousand garden gnomes from my gnome vendor for a dollar each, I cut them a cheque for three grand. That three grand essentially comes from the bank, so I pay interest on it - which of course I want to avoid. The best way to do that is for me to negotiate "payment terms" with you. The terms would be something like "net 60" which means once I receive the goods I have sixty days before I need to pay the three grand to you. The hope is that I can sell the three thousand units within two months (sixty days) so that before I need to pay the bank I have already made the money in sales to pay for the goods and I also get the profit from the sales. I then have the money to pay without borrowing and being charged any interest.

Over the past few years inventory has become a very big focus for investors when it comes to retailers. Companies who over-invest in tough-to-sell or unsellable stock are not attractive to investors because it will a) take large write-offs with company money to exit this inventory (money that could go to profits and in turn make the investor a return on their stock) and b) since banks will only give you so much money, a company has a cap on inventory costs – meaning bad buys eat up the dollars that could be spent on good, profitable, faster-selling products.

What does this mean for you?

- Don't flood a retailer with risky product. You don't want your brand to gain a reputation for having slow moving products.

- You also want to try to provide (if it works for your accountants of course) ample payment terms – this could win you the battle with another competing brand.
- Be supportive when I ask you to help move through some slow-moving goods. Don't live on "hope" when you sell products to me – if it's not selling after a few weeks or months don't cross your fingers and hope it will miraculously start selling to plan – buyers want "partners" who want product to sell through and not vendors focussed one hundred percent on just sell-in. These vendors don't last long – support product to sell smoothly so it doesn't become an inventory nightmare for everyone. Besides, if I don't sell it – I don't buy any more from you and long-term I'm guessing that doesn't work well for you or the manufacturer.

Vendor Funding

Vendor collections or "vendor funding" (different retailers have different terms for this) are the monies collected from vendors either in credit notes, payment agreements, back-end programs or other forms. These collections are important to keeping the lights on – they often offset charges the company incurs, and those charges associated with my category will show up on my P&L.

For example, if I charge you ten thousand dollars for a bulk stack of potato chips in the main aisle of all my stores for the month of October then I get you to sign off some document, have some back-up email, or something stating legally that you have agreed to do this. Once this activity has been done you owe me a cheque or debit note, or the funds are deducted from what we owe you for your product (we buy fifty thousand dollars of chips and when we cut the cheque we give you forty and keep the other ten for the bulk stack fees based on our agreement). There are many different ways this is handled depending on the retailer.

In the scenario above that ten thousand dollars goes into my P&L under "vendor funding" along with many other activities I may have money coming in from: end features, display allowances, listing fees and many other money grab opportunities we come up with. Some retailers may include advertising fees in this line or they may have a separate bucket for that.

Another common form of collection is a "back-end program" which will be part of your "vendor agreement" or "vendor contract" (again, each retailer may have different terms for all these things). All retailers will have some sort of legal agreement between the retailer and the vendor going over the rules of engagement and also detailing any programs and payments that are agreed upon. For example you could have: your payment terms, co-op (advertising) funds to cover off the cost of ad space, volume rebates, freight allowances, warehouse costs, labour fees and so on. These are all part of the cost of doing business and are important to pay attention to. You are judged as a vendor not just on the products you sell, but on what money I make from you when all is said and done. Here is a tale of two vendors:

	Vendor A	Your Company
Gross Margin %	36%	32%
Program %	4%	10%
Total %	40%	42%

In this example your company loses out on the very-visible and very important gross margin game BUT you have a much healthier back end program so overall YOU are the more profitable vendor partner for me!

Freight

Freight costs can come at a company in many different forms. One example is when you run out of an advertised product and are forced to send overnight couriers from the DC to each store that is out of stock. Not letting the customer down is the most important thing, but that direct shipment to the stores will cost you hundreds or thousands of dollars (depending on number of stores, type and size of product, and distances from the DC). The P&L will have a freight budget, but it probably does not leave room for these types of last-minute issues. Collaborative planning with the buyer can insure there will be less need for these types of extra costs to be incurred. The buyer may call you and ask you to ship the product from your warehouse to their stores – meaning YOU will have to cover the costs.

My P&L is everything I work for and each line is important. I have my top line sales and a bunch of other lines that greatly affect how much money I make at the end of the month. For simplicity let's say my P&L was as simple as the numbers below (which I wish it was as these are only a few of many lines I contend with):

Line	Actual	Budget	Difference
Sales $	6,200,000	6,000,000	200
Margin Rate %	32%	32%	
Product Gross Margin $	1,984,000	1,920,000	64
Vendor Funding $	10,000	8,000	2000
Profit $	1,994,000	1,928,000	2064
Shrink $	-2,000	-1,000	-1000
Markdown $	-600	-600	0
Ad cost $	-4,000	-4000	0
Other Marketing Cost $	-5,000	-5,000	0
Freight $	-3,000	-1,500	-1500
		Total +/-	-236

In this example I missed my month by $236. I was over in profit by exceeding my vendor funding line and being up slightly in sales, but I failed to control my shrink and freight costs and it cost me the profit I had gained. This is why all those other programs and controls of inventory and profitability are so important to cover off and try to structure your program around - because if you don't I will need to find someone who will, as senior leadership will not accept negative P&L's on an ongoing basis.

So you can see that, not surprisingly, financials are what makes my world go round - so you need to understand my needs and challenges and pitch me plans that cover off these important pieces of the equation. Ask the buyer what they need and how their financials get measured...explain your plan in those terms. It will sound a lot better to the buyer if your assortment, margins and display plans are laid out in a document showing how it will benefit their top line, bottom line and cut dollars off their shrink number – imagine how impactful that would be and how hard it would be to say no to. It shows you care about delivering the same goals the buyer has and it may be the only time they have ever been pitched that way – meaning YOU stand out as the salesperson who cared the most about their agenda!

"I appreciate a salesperson that runs/requests selling information, analyzes the information, and comes to you with an action plan on how to minimize risk and build on opportunities. I also appreciate it when they show a strong knowledge for my business and have good solutions on how to make it better." - A Senior Buyer at Old Navy

4

Understanding a Buyer's Mentality

Most buyers do not have God complexes, as many of you may believe. We are just business people trying to do the best at our job. We do wield a heavy sword for sure, depending on our categories and how big we are as a part of the market. Sadly there are buyers out there who choose to take advantage of their buying power. That is unfortunate and I don't operate that way, but you may run into a buyer who does so be prepared for it.

These "power-hungry" buyers love to keep you under their thumb – intimidate you, squeeze you, put you in the "panic zone" and dangle purchases over your head to get what they want. Unfortunately you may not have a choice but to play their game, but there are a few things you can do to make life easier:

- Make sure your bosses are fully aware of what you are dealing with. Some buyers may cross far too many lines and can be toxic to their employers – in extreme cases it is important to the business for your senior leadership to identify concerns to the buyer's bosses. Barring that situation, at least your bosses know what you are dealing with and can back you up in situations where you have to say no to some of the buyer's demands.
- If a buyer is a "grinder" – one that constantly grinds every price down they are presented with, you will need to start going in higher than you were planning to on cost so they can play their game and grind you down to where you were planning to be in the first place. This

47

often satisfies the need for power-hungry buyers to "win" the battle of wills. We know that vendors do this, so be careful how much of it goes on.

- Be their best friend. It is an ego thing so play to it – pretend to hang on their every word, show some fear now and again, ask them a lot of questions that allow them to feel like the brains of the operation. You are still in control of what you are doing (remember that) so there is no harm in playing along with their need for control. If you were going to give them a ten percent discount anyway, let them feel like they bullied you into it or you are doing it because you want to make them happy – they will eat it up. I am not saying to necessarily swallow your pride, but in some cases you need to choose between playing along or perhaps doing no business.

You will get some buyers that act tough but are not. Buying is not for the faint of heart – nine times out of ten it's a cut-throat, high-pressure, ulcer-producing stress factory and buyers of all personality types end up in this world – including quiet, shy, polite people who most of the time are forced to be who they are not and act the part of the big bad buyer.

These individuals are much easier to deal with, but will confuse you here and there with the odd, unexpected tantrum, tougher-than-usual demands or wild swings in the plans. Take these with a grain of salt – they are not always signs that you did something wrong, rather they may be the end result of that buyer being pushed by their boss to be tougher (to fit the "mould" of a typical buyer). Every company wants their employees to fight tooth and nail for every dime and most retailers love to see buyers hammer away at vendors to get the most out of them.

Times are changing though. Many retailers are finally realizing that long-term growth and sustainability comes from strong partnerships with suppliers. As many categories become commoditized, as more and more competitors get into various categories looking for additional revenue streams, it means a manufacturer has many options these days when it comes to where and how they sell their products. Take for example laptop computers – a category five to ten years ago that was owned by the specialty computer stores and big box electronics stores (because if you are going to spend a thousand dollars and not have an out-of-date model in six months you want expert advice on what gigabytes and RAM you need). Fast forward ten years later and you can buy a laptop that has more guts and power that you may ever need for three hundred bucks on any no-name web store shipped to your home for free. That big box electronics retailer has lost a lot of their buying power and can only hold on by ensuring they are a strong partner of the manufacturer.

This breeds the smart, talented relationship-savvy buyer. This is a buyer who understands the market, knows product and trends, understands the need for relationships that last and works hand in hand with you. Does this sound too good to be true? This buyer is actually quite common in this retail age and this is one you want to keep as a fan of yours. You need to keep up with their level of knowledge – they will not have as much respect for salespeople who are not in tune with their products or the market. They don't like being told they are wrong about things (like any buyer), but they are open to new ways to drive business or new product ideas. They expect that they can go to you for answers. They like the win-win situation.

The last type of buyer is going to be the rookie. These are the "green" kids who are unsure of themselves, make mistakes and fumble through a lot of things. This doesn't make them bad at what they do — it just takes some time (typically a year or two) to learn all the many ropes of the business (as you can tell from this book — it's not as easy as it may seem). Buying takes skill and a certain type of person to be great at it, so odds are the rookie buyer was put in this role, managing hundreds of thousands or millions of a company's money, because someone felt they had the characteristics that will make them a good buyer - so bear with them and help them as much as you can. They will remember the help you gave them and you never know — they could end up in a power position someday that may benefit you.

You need to know who you are dealing with so let's look at the possibilities (which could be a combination of two or more):

Rookie — just starting out, will be a rough road — help where you can and you will be rewarded

Grinder — their only play is to beat you down on cost — they become predictable so play to their style

Ego-maniac — they want to control you and have a need to win at all times — tread lightly and make it seem like you are their best friend

Frazzled — this buyer just doesn't have what it takes to handle the non-stop world of buying — they are unorganized, lack communication skills, have bad time management and are typically very unsure of themselves. Do what you can to keep them on track but be very cautious – don't get caught by their sloppiness and leverage their teammates or bosses for information or assistance

Run-of-the-mill – this us your everyday buyer – no major issues, no extremes (good or bad), does what they say they will most of the time, makes the odd mistake but hey, we are all human – keep a good working relationship, get to know them better personally as they tend to be friendlier and avoid being too in-your-face with these buyers – they are good to you until you get on their nerves

Guru – knows the business, analytical, strategic – they want to partner so do the same while insuring you know as much as they do

Dishonest – it depends how you do business, but this stuff never ends well for anyone – there will be those people who take advantage of their buying power and look for personal gain outside their company – kickbacks, free goods, trips, favors...some vendors deal that way – if you don't, then stay very clear from any of this talk

Uninterested – this person is not in the game mentally and is probably looking for another job – make sure you cover yourself and your business as these people will be sloppy and may not be around the next day – make sure your business would be in tact with the retailer if that happened

Retiree – they are on their way out, they have slowed down – at the same time they are well-respected by their peers so keep them happy until you hand them their retirement gift

The Next Vice President – this is an easy one – whatever it takes to make them happy do it – know your business, be professional and most of all – be that person that helps them get to the next level – trust me, you will not be forgotten!

There are thousands of retail buyers in North America – and every one of them is different. Sorry if you have one or two now that you deal with that are painful to work with – this will not always be the case, so don't paint everyone with the same brush – feel them out early and try to peg down who they really are and how to best handle their personality.

Buying or Rejecting?

Buyers can be very hard to read unfortunately. How nice would it be to have a sales-meter device that measured the buyer's willingness to say yes to listing the product? That of course does not exist, but there are ways to read their speech and body language. Here are only a few of many things to watch for to help you gage where you are with them:

Signal	What it may mean
Buyer has arms crossed and looks angry or bored	They are not buying into what you are pitching – so you may need to shift your approach. It may just be a technique the buyer uses however - to not show their cards so they can talk you down in price later
Buyer really grills you on the product and every little detail	This is not necessarily a bad thing – it often shows they are interested in it - as they would not waste their time with twenty questions if they were just going to say no anyway. Their questions may mean they are interested but want to see some changes to the product

Buyer responds to your pitch with the phrase "I'll think about it and let you know"	Most of the time this is their way of being nice and not crushing you on the spot. For newer buyers who are not comfortable yet with saying no in person they may use this to buy themselves some time so they can email you your no. In some cases a buyer may truly not have decided – give the buyer some time and then follow up or try to add to the pitch to close the sale
Buyer stomps on the price you quoted with a phrase like "there is no way I'd buy that for that price!"	This is their lead-up to grinding your down on price. Remember that few know the business and market like the buyer - so ask them to explain why and see if they have a strong argument or they are just one of those buyers who grinds the vendor on every cost
Buyer repeatedly compares your product to another in the market or in their assortment	This may signal that they already have their sights set on buying another brand's product or sticking with one they already assort – you need to read into this and go on the defensive by showing why yours is the better choice
Buyer seems genuinely interested in the product and the prospect of selling it in their stores	Obviously this is where you want to be – but don't assume anything or let the happiness fade – close the sale right away and get talking about quantities before they change their mind
Buyer says no	I may be way off base here but I think this means they don't want it. Having said that, you need to find out their concerns, what you could do to change that answer and fight to get them to change their mind if you can

Spending

One thing to remember is that a buyer always has that vendor funding line of their P&L (as explained in the last chapter). This means they are constantly searching for a way to get extra funds over and above (often referred to as "O&A" or "MDF" for Marketing and Development Funds) and you have to watch how you work with them. Here are some examples:

Free Spending – if you always say yes to every proposed fee you are for sure going to be the buyer's favourite, but this can be costly to you and guess what...you have to live up to that reputation – the next year the buyer will expect you shell out the same dollars or you will look like you are being less supportive to the business in the next year. You also may have to say no to some funding (because you blew your budget by saying yes so much!) and now the buyer is going to be concerned why suddenly you don't want to support like you were before

Planned Spending – this is the comfort zone you want to be in: establish a dollar amount at the beginning of the year and manage it well. Make the buyer aware of the dollar figure (with a buffer of course) so there are no false expectations. A good buyer will plan out the purchases and funding activities to start the year with you. Based on what you know you can handle, perhaps put a percentage to a purchase number eg: ten percent funding for ads, space fees and other activities based on a ten million dollar forecast = one million dollars in funding. At this point you bake a plan of those activities you will support that will drive the most business. Don't sign up for things that are just a "money-grab" by the buyer – be convinced it's a worthwhile activity – your bosses will want to know where their money is going. Plan a buffer in your funding (eg: you actually have been allowed to spend twelve percent so save the two percent for a rainy day – guaranteed a smart buyer will try to eclipse the ten percent with something or something will come up that you will need to overspend)

Non-spender – you don't want to be seen as cheap. Unless you are one of the few manufacturers who has a product so hot it sells itself, you will need to fund something at some point. Buyers will decide a lot of times on a vendor partner or product based on the funding model. Will this vendor support discounts to help move product? Will they share in the pain of exiting the product if it's a dog? If you are seen as unsupportive then it will hurt you down the line. You can keep things tight, but throw a bone here and there to make it look good and make sure the buyer knows you have limited funds if you truly do – they may be ok with that and it's worse if they expect ten thousand dollars for a program and you toss them two hundred dollars

In order to sell effectively to a buyer you need to know the type of buyer they are. You need to know their style, their mentality, what things are important to them. Spend some time thinking about this from early meetings and tailor your approach to how you think they would want you to be. It sound a bit sad and pathetic, but a good salesperson plays these games well and you should make sure you are one of them. There is nothing wrong with stroking a buyer's ego or making them feel like you are always on the same page even when you are not. It will go a long way and will pay off in the long run.

"I was a buyer for a major retailer when a revolutionary product first came out and I asked the manufacturer for money to put it in my weekly flyer – they basically said to me 'this is the hottest product on the planet and we can't make enough to satisfy world-wide demand...why would we give you money to advertise it – we created the demand already.'" – A former buyer for Best Buy

5

The World Wide Web

What if I said to you that I had no room in my assortment for your product but how about we throw it online and test it out? Most of you would take that as "sorry, you lose – here's your parting gift," but fifty percent of the time…ok maybe twenty…it's not a way to demote your product.

Over the years the World Wide Web has rapidly changed retail. Now you can buy just about anything online, cheaply (due to little or no overhead costs) and get it delivered to your home quickly. You could become a recluse ordering everything you need to survive for a year never leaving your home – including buying this book and reading it over and over as entertainment. Now billions of dollars are done online with the Ecomm giant Amazon leading the way. It's no longer such a bad thing to get listed only online with a retailer.

When a buyer says no to a product it means they a) don't believe in it, b) feels they already have something better or c) they truly don't have the space or open inventory dollars to bring it in, even if it's a great product. So you should embrace an alternative, albeit less desirable, placement – what do you have to lose? We do use the phrase "let's test it" to throw a small bone to a vendor we feel bad rejecting, but there is some truth in the statement that if it does show promise online we will relook at it. I have seen products banished to the web do more online sales than some of my regular assortment items and I cannot ignore that – especially if I have an astute salesperson highlighting the performance, constantly hoping for a shot at the big leagues.

The web can help build brands and get people interested in products – whether that is an item only sold online, or one that is both in stores and on the website. How often do you find yourself researching a product online before you go buy it in a store (or simply buy it right there online)? The web is now the number one marketing vehicle in the world and every bit of exposure helps.

"The number one source of traffic to a retail store is from their retail website, and the number one source of traffic growth to retail sites is from Google search results," says an Online Manager at Best Buy. "In fact, Google will soon drive over half of the traffic to the top retail sites. Leading retailers know this, and they should know how to ensure that they appear near the top of those search results. My advice to vendors would be work closely with your retail partner so that they are ranking near the top of the Google search page when customers are searching for your products."

If you sell a revolutionary TV remote (that is maybe too revolutionary for most retailers to put in their line-up) and Best Buy, the kings of consumer electronics, offers placement on their website - you would jump at the opportunity. Why? Because the majority of Americans looking for a better way to control their TV are going to key in "TV remotes" into the search bar of bestbuy.com and voila – your super remote will be there.

Savvy buyers are catching on to web trends and maximizing its power. They can see how many units your remote is selling each week - and if they are really in tune with things (but many of us are too busy to get this deep into things unfortunately) they will see what kind of attention it gets through click-throughs (stats on how many people clicked their way to your product) or how many times it was searched for.

Google is a very valuable tool to find products and when you are on a major retail website you have a better chance at showing up when someone searches for TV remotes in general. You can actually pay Google to get to the top of the list and drive sales to the product and then use the web traffic statistics to woo buyers into assorting your product. If you had five thousand people in a week click through to your TV remote on your company website it shows a lot of people are interested. If your website sends those customers to bestbuy.com to buy it you drive more web sales and hopefully the end result is in-store placement based on your huge cyber success.

"Retailers know that their future is dependent on their ability to adapt to a growing majority of customers using connected devices for all stages of their purchase process – from product research, to price comparison in the store aisle, to ultimately making purchases," notes an Online Manager at Best Buy. "Leading retailers are in a race to fundamentally shift all aspects of their business by adjusting their strategies to ensure that they remain accessible and relevant to the 'connected customer.' Many of these programs are so new that they may not be yet fully monetized. My advice to vendors would be to make a point of being the guinea pig for these programs. Get in on the ground floor by building strong relationships with the key contacts in the retailer's online business that are responsible for developing and executing these tactics."

"Utilize A+ content; post a logo, use multiple images, video, PDF data sheets and set up product pages strategically when publishing content on the webpage," adds an Online Buyer at Sears Holdings Corporation. "For example, use bullet points and be clear with features and benefits while implementing key search terms within descriptions for search optimization. This is key - and whether or not they buy it on the site or on another site that supplies the customer with a better price or offer, the vendor gets the sale, because the customer is buying "their" product."

Find out what web marketing vehicles the retailer has – just like you would if you were looking to market in stores and in flyers or newspaper ads with them. They may have big online sale events or special areas or programs on the site to highlight products and get more customer interest. Go on to most retail websites and you will see "banners" all over the site – blocks at the top, side or bottom of the pages that call out products or events that you may be able to secure for your product. These banners are where most internet advertising is done and automatically our eyes focus on them like we find a sale sign in the grocery store aisle. You will need the exposure in a lot of categories as the web often houses a wide selection for most categories on retailer's online sites and navigating through a hundred different coffee mugs to find the one you want can be painful. If your brand is AAA Coffee Mugs Inc., then the customer sorting the long list of products alphabetically is your friend, but if you are in the mid-price range and they sort lowest price to highest they will see fifty other mugs before they see yours...you get the point.

If you have your own product website make sure you are not setting your prices differently than the retailers you sell to are – some companies do this and if your price is lower it makes the retailer look like they are ripping their customers off. If your website is not transactional (you can't buy from it) then you will want to make sure you direct the customers researching your product on your site to your key partners. You may want to strike a deal with one main retailer that you will drive your web traffic to their site or note that customers can buy the product in those stores.

Facebook, YouTube and other social media sites are great drivers of awareness and purchases and should be fully embraced by all manufacturers and retailers. They are sites with millions of eyes looking at them daily and where many people learn about new products, what is hot, what is not and what to buy – and many activities are free to do to drive your brand message. You can work with the retailer on some joint ventures or again, tag the retailer in your social media campaigns.

When you get going with a retail partner, get to know their team – marketing, store design and web teams especially and find out exactly what they can offer and what the fees are, if any, to participate. That online manager will give you far more information and insight than the buyer will – that is their job and you can also get the web statistics from them to help decide if the web activities are a good investment. Getting behind the web marketing is key now and even more as time goes on – by embracing it and putting investment here you show the retailer that you understand the power of the web and its far-reaching potential. As a buyer I would worry about a vendor who ignores the online world – it shows they are out-dated and not easily able to adapt to change.

"As eCommerce grows, the opportunity to reach more people globally grows as well. The internet is the gateway to get the product out there. Consumers are using brick and mortar as a showroom (remember Service Merchandise?) and utilizing the internet as a resource to find a product that meets their needs while finding the best price and opportunity to buy it more conveniently (e.g. via free shipping, an affiliate coupon offer or Google shopping). We are constantly explaining this to vendors and getting them excited about building their business online."
– An Online Buyer at Sears Holdings Corporation

6

Go To Market Strategies

I have your products in my store now, but many products won't perform without that extra push – some kind of marketing to the consumer to either drive sales or at least let them know it exists in my stores. Every buyer has a "market strategy" they use to guide them on what activities to leverage to maximize sales. They know how much space in newspaper ads or their corporate circular (flyer) they will have and what other means they can take advantage of.

A marketing plan on a new computer mouse may look like this:

- ¼ page in July 19th flyer with headline announcing new product
- Launch at same time online on home page
- ROP in local newspapers the following week with industry reviews of product
- In-store demo through first two weeks of launch by vendor reps
- Train each staff member on product through webinar
- Set up contest for staff to reward top sales people
- Do online customer contest with alerts on website and also Facebook

This plan is typically a list of all the actions that will be taken on the product or line of products – it could also be for a brand or an entire product category. It is the mission statement on achieving sales and is often used to delegate out the various tasks needed to roll each piece of the puzzle out. You can be a part of this plan and help shape it and influence it – offer up suggestions on what can be done or ask to review the marketing plans around your products and see if you agree or have valuable input to make it better.

After the launch plans there should also be a regular marketing plan. This plan varies in detail from buyer to buyer and category by category. Certain retailers may also have different levels of marketing plans – some working on short-term plans and some long-term. Short-term plans may be on a month to month basis or even weekly as a buyer draws up their flyer plan three weeks in advance based on their business needs at the time (if their flyer lead time is three weeks out). Long-term plans range in length, but a buyer may plan out a quarter at a time or even have their entire years plan in place to start the year if possible. A full-year plan may be difficult as retail is an ever-changing beast. They may have an idea of what they would like to see and have actual plans landed (what products, what price strategy, what online plans etc) for three to six months and the next six months after that may be more of a rough idea. These longer-term plans are easier to ask for adjustments to if needed, but I would suggest working hand in hand with the buyer from day one on the entire plan.

There are several parts of the marketing plan to consider:

Category Strategy

The category strategy is the overall plan for a group of products. It will be a more high-level strategy that guides the finer details. It may look like this for a buyer who does Pre-School Toys:

1. Grow share in pre-school electronic and computerized toy segment
2. Train staff at annual training event on how to demo electronic toys
3. Increase gross margins in building blocks category by five percent
4. Reduce licensed character toys by one section and grow electronic toys by one section
5. Grow share in stuffed animals segment by two percent
6. Reduce sku count in dolls and accessories by ten skus

The example above has some measurable targets included in it and remains quite high-level. This part of the strategy is not very easy for you to influence but it's not impossible – it should be built on market research and business needs. You can always make suggestions to the buyer on what could be some of the focus for the year, but ensure you do not come across as being pushy – use market trends and any other statistics you can find to make your case. If the retailer grew five percent in electronic toys last year, the industry grew ten percent during the same period and your company is predicting a further twenty percent growth this coming year then you should highlight this to the buyer and suggest they could really make a big sales jump in this category based on that information. If the buyer has it in their overall strategy for big growth and your company is making a huge push on it as well you can better align your plans. If it is not in their plans and something else is a priority then you may find it hard all year to break into the buyers plans and get their full attention.

Knowing the buyer's plans in as much detail as they will share is very advantageous. In the above example you would know which categories they are looking to grow and reduce and where they are putting their money and efforts. The example shows the buyer has high hopes for electronic toys – maybe there are several key things you can partner with them on in that category – training, demo displays, volume buys etc. Get them excited about how you can help them reach their strategy goals!

Advertising Plans

As we all know, flyer advertising is a big sales driver – but you have to be smart about it. If you are paying money to a retailer (either in back end dollars or paying per ad) to put your products in their flyer that will hit hundreds, thousands or millions of households – you need to make sure you are not at the mercy of a buyer who has not thought through the best ad plans. In our busy world there are often things that we cannot do one hundred percent – advertising, with its major importance in many categories, was never one I let slip. You need to make sure your product doesn't fall into the "toss it in to fill the page" category.

A good buyer methodically plans out their advertising plan – mix of products, price points, traffic drivers, savings claims, new product launches and many other key metrics of a strong ad plan. Say I buy tools for a major home improvement chain. I have a lot of competitors and I need to get a leg up on them every single week. I do my research and know that hammers are where retailers are drawing in traffic with hot pricing. I also know that my biggest competitor has a really hot close-out deal on ten piece screwdriver sets that is getting a lot of attention. I also know from my market statistics that there is a big shift from standard levels to laser levels. So now I can start planning some ads. It might look like this if I get four products in the flyer:

1. I have to have a hot hammer deal so I go 6.99 on my basic hammer sku since I have seen many other retailers go to this price

2. I don't have the same ten piece screwdriver set, but I do have an eight piece. The competitor's set is ten pieces for 19.99 so I know I need to equal the 2.00 per screwdriver - so I go 15.99 on my eight piece

3. I then add a spot to a cool new laser level that has features on it that no other product in the market has – I make sure it's loud and clear that this is the best one to buy

4. For my fourth and final spot I have to think profit since I am taking a hit on a couple of the products (unless there is a sell-through allowance on my eight piece screwdriver set and opening price point (OPP) basic hammer where they become profitable). Seeing as I am not making much on the basic hammer I will put a heavy-duty hammer with lifetime warranty at 12.99. So I get to show the market that I too can compete on the 6.99 hammer business - but for only six dollars more you can jump up to a much better hammer

There are many strategies at play in the above ad scenario:

*   I always need to convince my customer that they can get the best price shopping at my store – today's consumer is very price-conscious and very few retailers can get away with over-pricing or carrying only high-end price point products (although there is still a

market for those). This is called "price perception" and I do that with my 6.99 basic hammer

- Let's say I make thirty percent margin rate on my basic hammer at 6.99 – that's 2.10 profit dollars for each unit sold. Let's say the product is normally 9.99 at fifty percent margin and now I am at thirty percent at the discount price – this is a descent margin rate for a deeply discounted item, but there are two problems: my average selling price (ASP) is now down (I will explain this further down) and my profit dollars per unit sold is down. I make 2.10 per unit on sale but at full price I make 5.00 a unit. If I sell twenty a week normally at full price I make 100.00. On sale I increase my sales to thirty-five so I make 2.10 x 35 = 73.50. I would have been better off, profit-wise, to leave it at full price - but I needed to gain price impression so it had to be done

- In the above scenario I could ask my vendor for support dollars to lower my cost to 4.00 (a 1.00 sell-through per unit sold) then I would make 3.00 per unit x 35 units = 105.00 and voila...I increased profit

- If I cannot get the support, which I could not for my flyer, I added the second "step-up" hammer sku into the flyer with the hopes that some of those thirty-five customers who would buy the basic hammer would see the benefit in trading up. If I have commission sales people I could direct them (in communications or through a monetary incentive (often referred to as a "spiff")) to try to talk every customer coming in for the basic hammer to buy the heavy duty one for just six dollars more (often called "upselling"). Say my cost on the heavy duty one is 7.00. I make 6.00 profit at 12.99 on it. If I convinced just ten of those thirty-five people who were buying the basic hammer to shift to buying the heavy duty hammer my total profit picture would look like this: 25 x 2.10 profit = 52.50 on the basic hammer and 10 x 6.00 = 60.00 on the upsell model for a total of 112.50...I have rescued my profit and I still planted the seed in the customers head that I have the lowest priced hammer in the market – which I want them to think of when they want a different tool – they may assume I also have the lowest price on other things (again, price perception)

- My fancy laser level showed customers I have the latest greatest technology too – not just cheap hammers, and if I get some people interested in buying this at 99.99 I grow my ASP, sales and profit dollars in a big way
- My last spot – the eight piece screwdriver set put the screws to my competitor (pardon the pun) by finding a way to deflate their big ten-piece close out deal they were so proud of

Average selling price (ASP) is the calculation of all the actual selling prices of a single item or group of products through a given period of time. All the individual selling prices are added together and then divided by the sales units to get the average price. Here is an example:

I sell 100 of chocolate bar A at 1.00 each = 100.00 in sales

I sell 200 of chocolate bar B at 1.50 each = 300.00 in sales

So I sold 400.00 of the two chocolate bars and a total of 300 units

400.00 divided by 300 = 1.33 average selling price

ASP is important because even though you sell more units on ad at a lower price, you need to sell a certain amount to make up the top line sales dollars. The average price of a saw is 20.00. I sell 100 units a week and it's the only saw in my assortment in the saws category for my budget. If I sell my 100 units of my 20.00 saw I make my budget of 2000.00 that week. If I put that saw on sale for 15.00 then I need to ensure I sell at least 133 units (133 x 15.00 = 2000.00) to make my sales. I need to ensure a 5.00 discount will increase my sales by thirty or more percent or I miss sales.

As a vendor you need to be aware of all this, as you can work with your buyer to make the right (educated) decisions for what goes in flyer. You can allocate your funding to drive your new technology, heat up slow moving products or drive hot deals in ad. Do the math – and give your buyer the thought process behind your suggested ad skus and pricing.

Your company will be happy their money was well spent on the right products. They will also want them in the right times – if you sell luggage you want to concentrate your ad spending around peak travel times obviously. You need to know those peaks inside and out – and it's not good enough to just know the peak travel times, you need to know how far in advance the typical traveller PREPARES for their excursion. If you know spring break is the second week of March it really doesn't help you to have luggage on sale that week – they have already left! You want to be in flyer each of the two or three weeks leading up to March break - so when they come to the realization that they could use a new suitcase for their trip in two weeks your product is screaming to be bought in my flyer.

Ask the buyer what the "lead times" for advertising are – if the flyer is created four weeks out and ships to the printer two weeks before the ad hits the streets - you know you need to finalize the plan prior to the four weeks and make any last minute adjustments before the two week cut-off. Within this timeframe you want to cover your behind by making sure you have called your fellow account managers and made sure the product you are suggesting I advertise at 199.99 save $100 isn't 149.99 save $150 at my biggest competitor – this is part of what is called "channel management" and it is YOUR responsibility to make sure I don't pick up the phone when their ad breaks screaming bloody murder.

It is never too early to let me know you are going to be getting out of a product. We can both benefit from a final clear-out ad in a flyer or at least a lowered price. You may feel like keeping a product transition under wraps until close to the change-over will save you from supporting an ad, but it will cost you much more later when you want me to bring in your latest version and I still have tons of the old model left. So take the opportunity to get that last clean-up ad in and get through product.

Channel Management

Channel management is a concern for most buyers. Those that are in smaller retailers are concerned about what the big boys are doing with their leverage (store count and buying power with their volume). The big guys are worried about the little guys because they can be disruptive – slashing a price on a popular item and taking a loss to gain customer traffic. A two store chain slashing the price of a lawnmower and taking a loss on fifteen units costs that retailer minimal damage financially but wins over local shoppers. The big guy must react to save face with consumers and in their one hundred stores they will sell seven or eight hundred at a loss and that hurts much more. You don't want to see this happen to your product unless you had this plan worked out in the market, as the big chain's buyer will be on the phone immediately to you looking for money to cover their losses because you did not manage your retailers well enough.

Sure, you just sell product and give a list price and cost and put the rest in the hands of the retailers in most cases, but there has to be a level of trust with your buyers that they won't kill the price in the market. Some retailers are infamous nationally or regionally for their pricing practices or "creative marketing practices" with sketchy deals meant to get you in the door to sell you something else because they only had one unit per store. These "slimy" guys are unsettling to more trustworthy partners and if you decide to sell to them then that is your prerogative – but you have to be responsible for their damage.

It doesn't even have to be price – it can just be reputation. If a retailer is known for cheap, unreliable no-name garbage they sell in dump bins like a flea market and you sell them your latest TV model – the same one you just sold a thousand of to a nine hundred store highly-respected electronics chain, you may want to rethink that decision. That big chain that makes your product look good and is the reason your kids will go to college because of the big commissions you get from their gigantic monthly orders is going to bite your head off for putting your products into a chain that makes customers think it is a cheap piece of plastic. It's damaging to your product's reputation as a quality product and you are going to have to tell your kids that they will be flipping burgers the rest of their lives because the big chain's request to send every last TV back to you is going to reverse that commission!

Most retailers can play nice and many carry the same products, but if you are in a category that has the ability to be different in various retailers this can really help reduce the pain. You could give new products to some and a close out deal on last year's model to others (if they are ok with that), you can have different styles of a product that can be sold in separate retailers to avoid conflict, or you can give your top retailer an exclusive on a product where they are the only ones to have it for a pre-determined timeframe.

The exclusive is a tough one in a lot of cases – it really rewards a retailer, as it drives customers only to them to buy it and leaves everyone else out in the cold. This can be great to reward the top retailer or gain other listings, but watch that you don't alienate the other key accounts you deal with – they are not going to be happy if a) it is an in-demand hot product and b) there is no 'plan B' for them to compete with it. You have to be strategic and think of all the issues that may arise by giving the exclusive. You may want to grant a short window like thirty days from launch to one retailer – you can always claim the product was in short supply at launch and so you had to choose one retailer to initially launch the product with and the rest of your key partners will get it shortly. This isn't perfect because everyone wants to believe they are your number one, but it is giving them something – not just "sorry, I like them better so I gave it to them to rub in your face every day for the next thirty days."

The conflicts are many in retail so do all your homework when you decide your partners and strategies with assortment – it is hard to say no to someone on a product, and you still need to keep them happy. A huge part of your job is the balancing act: making everyone feel special at all times. Some you can take the risk that they will be angry if they have a history of stomping their feet every time they don't get what they wanted, but always come back with purchase orders for those they can get. But some buyers often use purchases as a weapon against you (it's the best weapon we have!) and you need to know if not opening up that hot product to them will cause them to react negatively and dump the skus you have with them in retaliation – it happens a lot...don't take chances and burn bridges.

One way around it is to offer a similar product line or deal. Like in my earlier example of the ten piece screwdriver set – my competitor had that as a close-out deal that I was not offered. I would be angry that my sales rep didn't come to me with that offer and instead chose to disadvantage me in the market. I would then tell my rep they are not a strong partner and go find a better deal with that rep's closest competitor (who I explained the situation to and said they could take over the assortment if they can beat the other guy's costs, because clearly the other guy was more interested in the business at other retailers...it's all part of the buying process to pit one vendor against another). If my rep had been up-front and said there was a hot deal going out to a competitor (you do not need to tell us who that competitor is unless we torture you and make you cough up the information) but said "but we want to give this eight piece set to you at a special price...I think you will win with this deal" then I would feel like I was being taken care of in the situation.

Another part of channel management is making sure each of your retail partners knows what's happening with your product in the market. I don't mean telling everyone what your plans are with each of their competitors, but no buyer likes surprizes – like walking into Costco to see three giant pallets of your top selling GPS for half of your price. It is not a requirement for you to share business plans in advance, but a strategic "heads-up" to a strong retail partner goes a long way – instead of waiting for the buyer to be shopping at Costco on their lunch hour and call you from his cell phone to scream at you for an hour. Deals happen – we all know they do and we know we are not going to get priority on all of them, but no buyer likes to be embarrassed in the market and our bosses scream at US for an hour when we do - so save us the pain and do what you can to at least warn us its coming - or think twice about doing it. If I need to constantly react to your half price deals in the market on a sku I carry from you every day (or a similar one) I may get tired of the battles and go find someone else to sell to me who is less disruptive.

I may also come to you as the vendor I think can compete on someone else's hot deal. In this case you may have the instinct to say no if it's a crazy deal, but this could be a big opportunity to get a bigger chunk of my regular business down the road. I am desperately seeking an answer to a deal out in the market that someone has – perhaps one of my own vendor partners. If you swoop in and save me with a hot offer it makes me look good in the market and in front of my bosses and I will remember how you came through. It may have meant your company made little to no money and/or you made zero commission, but the foot in the door or an elevated status with me may be worth the one-time hit. Perhaps you make a deal that you will support if I add a regular sku to the line – so you can recoup the loss using regular margin sales over time.

In the buyer's world we do love vendors who come through with the "killer deal" and if you do come up with that one-time deal to help me compete guess what...I will think you are capable of it all the time. So make sure you let anyone at my company who will listen, especially me, know that you took a loss on it just to be a good partner – kill the expectation up front that this will be a regular occurrence if it won't.

When it comes to giving us a heads-up on things happening in the market you do need to be very careful. You are going down a slippery slope if you get into sharing plans and strategies of competitors. We of course love finding out these things, as it is to our advantage and we want to crush them whenever possible, but I personally don't want to know from you. You may say "ya sure – like you wouldn't want to know in advance what your enemy is going to advertise on the front page of their flyer so you can beat them to it"...of course I would – but why I say I don't want to hear it from you is that it means your integrity is suspect, and I assume if you are telling me their secrets, you are telling them mine! I prefer to compete on the strength of my own plans – not my reactions to private information.

Some buyers are different of course and will want to know all the dirty details of what their competition is doing, so you need to be prepared for that as well. You may have it and willingly give it to them (to gain favour with them) and that's your call, or you may NOT want to play that game - so you need to know ahead of time what stance you will take if a buyer asks those types of questions. Most of the time the right answer is "I can't give out that information - as I would not give your plans to them," but it may be an uncomfortable situation so be sure you know how to handle it. Again, it's always good to keep your bosses aware of such requests and that you didn't break any rules or agreements (for example NDAs – Non-Disclosure Agreements) so if anything ever happens, where say a buyer is fired for such activities, your bosses know you took the high road.

Some pieces of information are fine to discuss – like the fact you gave the other guy the exclusive on a new launch product, but saying they bought three thousand pieces to put in flyer next Tuesday at 9.99 is privileged information. What works often as a middle ground is subtle hints that let the buyer know they need to change their plans so they don't get burned. For example, if you know that their number one competitor has a bike coming up in ad at two hundred dollars off, and you are planning upcoming ads together, you could simply say "you may want to increase your sale price to two hundred dollars as there may be someone else at that price in the market." This doesn't report specific privileged information – it is just directional and allows the buyer to make a change if they heed the warning. If they don't do anything, they cannot get angry at you when they get beat on the flyer price. If you are participating in ad planning with the buyer, you can try to find out from your company the general plans of each retailer and make ad recommendations to the buyer during your planning that avoid conflicts for that buyer and also the other retailers – ensuring your company stays in everyone's good books!

Sharing information up front is also helpful in advertising and planning the business. Knowing my lead time for ads is for example three weeks - try to let me know about price changes to your product in the market before my drop dead date to change the flyer. If you tell the market two weeks out and my competitor has only a two week lead time to go to print then I get beat by a week. You may have a certain date you can't release the information to buyers until – that is a special case, but you could forewarn me of an upcoming announcement and the timing, and I could at least prepare my teams for an online announcement or something other than in flyer. Then I can avoid looking like I'm asleep at the wheel in the eyes of the customer when the most revolutionary product in the history of toaster ovens emerges and my closest competitors announce it on the front page of their flyer - while I have no place to speak of it and look like I am not up with the latest products (a trait my loyal shoppers want from me).

Market Share

Market share is a buyer's proof that they are better than their counterparts at other retailers. This is the measure of what piece of the pie a retailer has in a given category. If I sold four hundred salad spinners last year and one thousand were sold in the entire country (market) then I had forty percent market share last year. Many retailers hold their buyers accountable to these published numbers and they can mean a lot:

- Growth shows I am taking share from my competitors
- It shows that our plans as a company or in individual categories are working – including capital dollars the company may have spent on new fixtures or a marketing plan the company devised
- Growth can show the skill of a buyer or team – it's essentially a report card (along with the P&L)
- It can also show the opposite and signal shortfalls in plans or buyer/team skills when it shows share decline
- It may also be telling to company executives when a buyer is struggling to hit their budget but they are

growing share beyond the anticipated rate – meaning perhaps the budget was set too high since I am taking share from all my competitors despite showing a shortfall to budget – perhaps we overestimated the market size when making the budget

As a supplier, you too may be measured by the same industry numbers and share position. You don't want to lose share among your competitors and you want to dominate as much of your category as possible – it means your company is making the sales and your competitors are not. So it makes sense to plan for a win-win partnership with the retailer. You know your goals and how much of the market you are trying to get – find out what my goals are and we can build the plan together.

If one of my vendors is a huge chunk of the market, but I am a tiny piece of their business it tells me that I obviously am not their go-to retailer and therefore I probably won't be the one getting all the hot deals and extra funding dollars. That may be true – but on the other hand, perhaps a bigger retailer has no more room to move the needle – perhaps they carry all your products and have them all over the store in the best areas...that means I may be the best opportunity for you. By growing business with me, because I do not carry all the products and have your skus hanging from my rafters, you have a greater chance of increasing your market share – especially if you can replace one of my other brands in your category and steal share from them. Now I may be where you want to spend your money and do some hot deals. If you explain your goals and how I can assist in getting you to where you want to be and it will bump me up in share over my last year's numbers – I am all for it. But there really does have to be something in it for me (share gains, extra support dollars etc) or you run the risk of me feeling like I'm just being used and abused.

Most share reporting services will give you all kinds of stats and figures to help you analyse the market (depending on what price you pay them usually) and it is a good idea to use these statistics to develop products and plans. If you know who the top retailer is in your category then it's a no-brainer to get your products listed with them – but you also want to know who is growing, who owns certain segments that may not be number one overall, who is sliding and may be a retailer you scale down skus with. You may even get regional share numbers – maybe there are big opportunities in Kansas and Oregon with a regional retailer who may not show up on a national level of reporting. Maybe a retailer is not on the radar but has aggressive plans to take over a category in the market by massive expansion of that category's space in store...you always need to be on the lookout for these things.

You may have noticed something throughout the book: that buyers are sensitive creatures who read a lot into each situation with salespeople and vendors in general. One of the greatest sources of frustration revolves around marketing and not losing out to our competitors. We all feel, whether big or small retailers, that we should be treated equally by our vendor partners. This isn't always going to be the case and frankly, it really doesn't make sense that a vendor would not favor a much larger account over the smaller one – but finding ways as a salesperson to keep things as fair as possible is important. Don't severely disadvantage your accounts versus other ones, and ensure you are in the know about what other account managers in your company are planning so their activities don't hurt you with your buyers. It's a significant source of buyer-vendor tension - so find ways to avoid marketing conflicts while driving strong plans with your buyers.

"Those who were most effective spent time in the stores and on my floor pad. They understood my strategies and what I was trying to accomplish. They also understood my competitors and what they were doing. They could identify my weaknesses. These sales people came to me and told me what need their product addressed in my assortment and where it should go on my floor. They did the thinking and solution finding for me. It made it very easy for me to make a decision and also gave me the ammo I needed to present to my superiors." - A former Senior Buyer at Target

7

Today's Forecast

Forecasting is one of the most important facets of the buying and selling process. Some retailers have sophisticated automated forecasting systems that generate the numbers for the buyer and inventory control teams, some companies have people in place other than the buyer to work the numbers, but many retailers put that task on the buyer – they select the assortment, determine how much it will sell (therefore how much to buy), how to market it to sell and deal with vendors for the life of the product until it is discontinued or "end of life" (EOL).

Within the above processes the buyer must ensure adequate supply to each store and online to satisfy customer demand. This means determining how much initial quantity to buy to fill each store – and what it takes to fill a store. For example:

- I assort a new three-pack of cherry-chocolate flavored gum (those are two things I am craving right now so I used them for my example – if it was closer to dinner time I might have used 'steak-flavored' gum)

- I have one hundred stores to launch this in

- I have one peg available for this product in my planogram/assortment

- I know that I can fit thirty packages deep on each peg based on the depth of the packaging

- I expect my sales per store per week to be approximately fifty

In the example above I can now determine my "opening order quantity"...

1 peg x 30 packages x 100 stores = 3000 units

So I need three thousand units just to fill my stores – but I need much more than that ordered because at fifty per store per week I will sell five thousand units in the first week. I only have room for thirty on my peg, but if I only give each store thirty they will all be empty before the end of the first week of sales – so I need to give them back-up stock as well to replenish the store with.

"Case packs" are important to the calculation – this is the vendor's carton size of the product. Some retailers send only full cases to stores and some break down the cases in their distribution centers (DC) so they can send smaller quantities at a time. This is important to know as a vendor – if I sell fifty a week and your smallest case pack is a box of five hundred and I ship stores full case packs then there will be a whole bunch of cherry-chocolate gum sitting in the back stockroom of each of my stores (ten weeks worth). This is especially important in confectionary/perishable categories where consumables have certain shelf lives and expiry dates. It is important to work with the retailer to get case packs to manageable sizes.

Say your case pack is twenty. I would likely send three case packs to each store in the initial shipment (sixty units total) –

which is thirty to cover the stock to fill the peg full (often referred to as "presentation stock"), the extra twenty to cover the first week's expected sales of fifty units and another ten units as a buffer in case cherry-chocolate is a bigger hit than anticipated. So in total I need six thousand units (60 units x 100 stores).

It doesn't stop there of course – I can't run out after one week so I need some back up to send my stores near the end of the week so they get more before they are completely out. Most retailers have defined metrics on this – often called weeks or days on hand (WOH/DOH) which simply means how much stock I carry at any given time to fill my sales needs.

Let's say I want to be safe and have enough in my DC to cover two weeks of sales on the gum. I also want the stores to carry two weeks worth at all times. My WOH would look like this:

Weekly forecast per store = 50

2 weeks forecast x 100 stores = 50 x 2 x 100 = 10,000

2 extra weeks in DC = 10,000

Total stock = 20,000 = 4 WOH

So for my opening order I need twenty-thousand units from you to get things rolling. You need to know this quantity so your company can go and secure that much stock for me so you don't short-ship me. As already mentioned – not having the stock I require is a very easy way to get in my bad books – this is how both of us get paid – by maximizing the sales opportunity – you to me and me to my customers. If you can't supply me then we both lose and I can't trust you to deliver what I need. I may start looking for a new supplier if you consistently have supply issues – that's just how business works.

The forecast is of extreme importance here though – I cannot get angry at you as a supplier for not having enough goods to deliver to me if I did not give you any advanced warning of what I actually need on an opening order or ongoing basis. As a salesperson you will inevitably run into the "why can't you get me stock" argument with a buyer – it will come up at some point in each of our long careers and this is your number one defense; not having line of sight to the retailer's needs. Of course this needs to be true...if you have been given accurate forecasts well in advance and told when you need the goods delivered by - then your best bet is to apologize, tell the buyer you will get it fixed and go yell at your supply chain people for making your company look like fools. But if there was never a forecast in place it's hard for a buyer to hold you FULLY accountable.

I use the word "fully" in the last statement because it is important for you as a salesperson to ensure that all the buyer-seller processes are running smoothly and keeping everyone in the loop on product needs is perhaps one of the most important. If you want to sell as much product to me as possible and want me to sell as much as possible to consumers you will take a vested interest in whether I have a forecast out to you regularly. Hold the buyer and their team accountable to get their forecast to you in a timely manner.

This forecast has many dimensions too – it's not just "give me twenty-thousand units every four weeks" – it's much more complex. Here are some key points to consider:

- I know how much I expect to sell each week and need to cover that, but I also need to include any ads that I am planning on running. I know for certain that I will get a lift in sales when I advertise so I need to request that extra amount to cover off the ad lift – otherwise I will over-sell my regular sales rate and be short product

- I have to know as a buyer what your "lead time" is (how long it takes you to produce the product and get it to me after I request it). Let's say a microwave takes sixty days to build in Asia and ship to the vendor's warehouse, then another five days to get to my DC. That is a sixty-five day lead time from the time I ask for a thousand units. If I need those thousand units for a flyer ad coming up in two weeks then guess what...not going to happen. But, if I am well planned out and, knowing your lead times, forecasted this to you that I would need these thousand units more than sixty-five days ago then we wouldn't have any issues. This is where being a cog in the ad planning wheel is also important – so you know what will be coming up and make sure there is a forecast in place for it

- Seasonality is another key factor. Sure my regular run rate on a television is seventy a week, but what about when students move into dorm rooms at back to school time? What about the big lift for holidays? What about all those people who just have to have the biggest flat panel imaginable to show off to their friends during their big Super Bowl bash? These are seasonal lifts and need to be properly forecasted, as neither of us would want to miss out on the extra sales

- You have to let me know when this item may be going end of life so that I can a) forecast it down to zero so I don't over-order and get stuck with a bunch of obsolete goods and b) I can start the forecast well in advance for the replacement product if there is one

Now, as discussed in other parts of the book, it is a shared obligation for us to manage the sku performance through the product life cycle. This means that I give the initial forecast to you and that is now the bar that has been set for that product to achieve as a run rate. If that product under or over-performs we have to deal with it together accordingly. Because of this you want to have a say in the initial targets of each of your products. If your product's performance and ability to stay active in my assortment is based on this weekly or monthly sales unit achievement then why would you not want to have a say in what that number is? You would be surprised at how many salespeople don't bother to even ask what that is. When you don't seek to participate I often wonder of you are mainly concerned with the big load-in order as opposed to the ongoing sales of the sku.

It may seem a challenge a lot of times to know enough about my business to help set the sales rate on a new item – you don't know the sales of similar skus in the assortment from my competitors, what my pricing may be, what you will be up against. But what you may know are things I don't; what the product sells per week with your other accounts, what past skus of yours that might be close in performance have done, what this product should do in the market versus competitive skus. If you contribute some of what you know (without revealing information I should not know about my competitors) and you enquire about my logic on my rough numbers, then we can both rubber stamp the final targets and both be happy with what we are signing up for. If you tell me you are happy with selling two hundred earmuffs a week and I am selling twenty you know I am coming back to you saying "how do WE get to our two hundred unit goal from twenty?" – I won't be slugging along at twenty a week too long and still keeping the product on my floors - as every bit of my real estate in my stores needs to deliver and slow moving skus are not something I'm going to ignore – especially if I'm struggling to hit my sales targets overall.

It is to your advantage and mine for you to be involved in the forecasting process for your products. The forecast holds you and I to a weekly or monthly sales quantity and if it's too low we will run out of stock – if it's too high we are going to be over-stocked and I will be coming to you for dollars or returns to get out of my bad situation. A lot of salespeople don't ask enough questions in the forecasting process – the best of them being able to make educated suggestions to the buyer to help them come to the best number. Ensure the right parties are getting together for collaborative forecasting.

"Most big retailers have vendor "partners" on site that have access to reports with their product. All vendor reps should be able to provide detailed analysis of their business/products; rate of sale, weeks of supply, TY vs LY etc." – A Buyer at Dollar General

8

Do This, Don't Do That

You have now learned several major things: what you should and should not do when trying to break into my world, how to approach your plans with me, how to tailor your plans to the things that drive me as a buyer (namely hitting my P&L) and how to identify what kind of buyer I am so you and I can get along wonderfully until our buyer-vendor marriage comes to an end.

Now I get to explain all the random stuff that comes up in my world that is within your control or would be useful for you to understand. These little tidbits of information can be the difference between landing my business (or keeping it if you already have it) and being rejected or dropped because you failed to understand the system. They are best described in the context of my annual business cycle.

Research

For two decades I have experienced many different sides of retail – buying, marketing, stores, operations, loss prevention, human resources...you name it and I probably have had some experience in it. It is helpful to have a well-rounded portfolio in the business because you need to understand the complete system to maximize one of the biggest cogs in the wheel, which of course is buying - where the wheel kind of begins.

I say that the process "kind of" begins with buying because it is all circular – I buy three products, say camera cases, and I put them in the store to sell. There is a green one, a black one and a blue one. They do their thing in the store all year and here I am ready to buy another three skus for the next year. If I'm a good buyer I of course don't just arbitrarily pick three pieces and ship random amounts out to each store – I need the history of the past year or two to make this year's decision.

I will look at two things first: what sold last year in my stores and then, provided I have access to the statistics, what sold in the market. I see that black and blue sold eighty percent of my sales and green was just twenty percent. So now I'm questioning green as a color choice. I research the market and find that the top colors in the market are black, blue and pink. I know now that I have a "gap" in my assortment and I replace my green with a pink case for the new selling cycle.

I expect that my top vendor partners can provide me insight into the market, so make sure your big presentations include market updates and predictions and tie your business plan into that information. I once gave a vendor a single spot on my shelf and asked them to choose between a new technology product and an old format barely hanging on. This company had just finished presenting me with industry trends showing the old technology was fading fast and the new was set to be the standard that year. Incredibly they chose the old technology because they said "we invented it twenty years ago and it's what we want to stand behind." I carried it for six months and then discontinued it and that vendor never saw product on the shelves again. The smart move would have been to say "we want to see you win in the new technology and we want to grow this segment as well...let's build our assortment and marketing plan around the hottest trend."

Where to Find New Products

I need to seek out a pink case, so I need to think of where I can get the best one. There are several avenues open to me: current vendor partners like the ones who sold me my black and blue cases, vendors who have pitched me in the past, ones I saw in ads, competitor's stores or online, maybe I Google search "pink camera cases" and see what comes up, perhaps I find an industry website like a photo equipment review site and do some research - maybe a site that showcases different products specifically from suppliers to buyers, maybe I fly to a trade show and shop around, perhaps I read a trade magazine, maybe I have a fellow buyer who does laptop bags that might recommend a vendor of theirs that has been a good partner and could make my pink goldmine sku. Exhausted yet?

As you can see there are many options, so ensure your marketing efforts out to buyers are comprehensive and cover as many of my research points as possible. This will get you noticed by buyers who don't know you exist, and also implant into the brains of those that know you already several impressions of your products so they say to themselves "hey, I remember seeing their product in a few magazines and websites."

If you are going to market to buyers I strongly suggest you do it right – for example, don't skimp on costs and put out a sad looking ad in a trade magazine. If you choose to participate in a trade show – make your booth look nice – there are many ways to make it look professional without breaking the bank. Cheap and cheerful won't attract a major retailer into your booth in a million years, unless they are asking if they can use your garbage can. We can tell small-time vendors from a mile away at these shows and even if you had the most innovative, cool new product a buyer will avoid you because your booth makes you look like you and the kids produce the product in your garage on weekends.

Tradeshows are a great way to attract business because they are typically held by an association of some kind that caters to your product group. This ensures that the timing of the show fits perfectly into the buying cycle. Be prepared to wow me – give it everything you've got! This is a golden opportunity.

My pet peeve about tradeshows (because I have been to about fifty so I am passionate about these things) is simple: please, I beg you, do NOT set a meeting with me at a tradeshow just to say you met with all your accounts. At my very first tradeshow I was not experienced enough to know to not clog my calendar with a bunch of meetings, and not leave any time to actually walk around the show floor and see new product (which is kind of the point). I had tied up all my time with meetings with existing vendor partners. This is fine if you have some top secret products to unveil for me at the show, but if I could have seen the line-up at your offices two blocks away from my headquarters back home you may be wasting my time. So during this first tradeshow I head over to one of my vendor's booths. I asked for my sales contact at the front of this large exciting-looking set-up and he proceeded to take me inside the booth in all its glory and offer me a seat at a small table off to the side. Then he sat there fairly silent - apart from some small talk for about five minutes until I asked him what the agenda was. He responded by saying "oh, we don't have any new products to show – but we wanted to make sure we sat with each of our key accounts during the show." This would be allowable if it was at least a chance to get to know the VP or president - but no, it was just him (who I talked to all the time back home) and I sitting staring at the well-decorated walls. Bottom line: time is money so please don't do this to you buyers!

Now I have done the tradeshow thing and I am prepared to make some educated guesses on what route to go. I choose your pink camera case and we are off to the races. I order a thousand units from you and they have a sixty day lead time from overseas...we are now in the waiting game.

Product Display

During that waiting game I am deciding where to merchandise the camera cases. I may have a permanent home with my photo accessories, but I would be open to the suggestion of a second facing somewhere else in the store – such as the checkout (cash register) lane. Most of the time there is going to be a fee system in place for secondary locations of products.

You brand new salespeople may ask why this is since there is no cost to having a peg on a counter in a store. The answer is simple...because someone else will pay it. Retail is all about the exposure of product to the consumer and, depending on the product, it will sell significantly more units when given greater exposure. Checkout lanes, main aisles, end features, sides of end features, clipstrips, profit panels and many other "special treatment" options are all much-sought-after spaces for vendors and so they will pay top dollar for that space – their reward being increased sales.

You should be questioning where your products are being merchandised – don't leave it to the buyer alone or you may end up at the bottom of the planogram (counter layout) where nobody looks. This obviously will not help sales and therefore you won't see too many repeat orders.

The customer reads a counter like they read a book: top to bottom and left to right. They are particularly drawn to product at eye level because we tend to walk around facing ahead of us and so any good retailer will take full advantage of this. The best in this business are the big grocery chains – they live and die by their ability to manipulate the consumer into buying what they want to sell (because it's a profitable sku or because they are getting money from the vendor to sell as much of it as possible).

When you walk a grocery store the store layout is often similar between each competitor (at some point a "best-in-class" was determined to which all others followed). You enter at the bread or deli where it smells great and gets your stomach wanting food, you snake your way through the aisles like a rat in a maze - which ensures to see every aisle, and you end at the milk - which is the most bought staple food in the business along with bread (so you start with bread and pretty much have to pass half or all of the store to get the milk...ah the beautiful mind games). But wait, as you walked the store you nearly fell over fifteen bulk bins in the main aisles and each counter has an end feature (endcap) of specials, so if you didn't snake your way up and down each aisle you still had to pass twenty endcaps. If you did a full-on weekly shopping trip down each aisle you were exposed to all forty endcaps. On each side of those endcaps may have been side racks (aka profit panels, sidewinders etc) with more useless trinkets you may think you needed, and on every single four foot section of counter there may have been clipstrips (plastic or metal strips that hang from the middle of the counter and house hangable "add-ons" that go with the product on the shelf eg: cat toys hanging by the cat litter section). Then when your cart is overflowing and you head to the checkout area you are faced with a bunch more garbage you can't help but grab.

I am a student of "impulse buying" or "customer shopping patterns." One of the great retail books ever written is Paco Underhills's *Why We Buy* – the bible of those in the customer mind game business. One of the more interesting things I learned from my time in retail came from a magazine vendor when I was overseeing a checkout merchandising project. They explained to me the method to how they display their magazines – it was so simple, but I had never stopped to wonder why they place things where they do. They almost always have two displays in each checkout lane to magazines – one at the end and one over the conveyor belt by the cash register. There are different titles on each display – the front endcap has magazines like ones targeted at future brides or home and garden publications – the theory being that you will be waiting in line and therefore have ample time to flip through a magazine and decide that you are interested and buy it. As you get to the register and unload your cart you are in the "pay and get the heck out" mode and therefore you are presented only with the quick-pick-up TV guide, gossip mag etc that you would likely always read - so you just grab it and add it to your purchases. Smart.

Merchandising is key – you wouldn't put sugary kid's cereals at the top of the shelf would you? No, you would put them at KID eye level so they see it in two seconds flat and spend ten minutes annoyingly begging their mom or dad for it until they cave in and throw it angrily in the cart. So don't let your product be shoved into the planogram anywhere where it will be doomed to collect dust. You will also want to make regular store visits through the year to make sure it has not gone from good placement to bad behind your back. You also want to look around the store for those golden opportunities to get a secondary display and suggest it to the buyer. Don't offer funding up front – suggest it in hopes they just see it as a good opportunity to sell more of a good product - but work with them if there is a fee.

On top of preferential placement on the planogram you may also suggest a displayer or fixture of some kind that accentuates the product on the shelf. Like in a car dealership, they display all the cars, but there's always that one shiny new one spinning around on a pedestal in the middle of the showroom – perhaps your product lends itself to having a fancy display that shows off its features. Many products need to be touched, gripped, seen or heard in order for the customer to make their decision. Would you buy a TV for two thousand dollars without seeing how clear the picture is first? You may want to have some signing that tells the customer the key highlights of the product as well. If it will sell more product then buyers are usually all for it – barring their corporate display guidelines (many retailers have internal groups that approve signs and fixtures to make sure they fit the "look and feel" of the store and company messaging - so ensure anything you do gets approved). The buyer may also have agreements in place with other vendors for their display space so push for the fixture as much as possible, but let it rest of you keep getting told no.

Demos and Training

Another sales helper you can offer, depending on your category of product, is in-store demos. Any extra sales help a buyer can get is helpful. In a perfect world the sales staff would all be eager, career-focussed go-getters that only want to deliver the best customer experience – but we all know that is a fantasy world fifty percent of the time or worse, and we get the lazy student who only wants to run the clock and talk to their buddies all shift while ignoring the shoppers with fists full of cash.

Setting up demos of products for customers helps drive awareness of your product as well as sales through my cash registers, so it can often be a win-win situation. One store could sell fifteen vacuum cleaners on a demo day on a product you were averaging ten a day in all stores normally. It wasn't selling because nobody knew by the packaging just how powerful this thing was, but the demo showed fifty people an hour what it did – fifteen bought it based on that demo in that day, and the many other customers who didn't buy now have it in their minds that if their Suckmaster 3000 ever dies they are headed back to buy your model.

There is another great side effect to the in-store demo...employee education. The person in that area of the store who is supposed to sell your vacuum may not have any idea all the cool things it does, but when they have watched your demo guru in action their entire eight hour shift they certainly know every pitch in your vacuum selling book.

Another option is to send a trainer into stores to get them up to speed on the product. Maybe on a day where a few staff are working (for better efficiency) they can go in and spend ten harmless minutes going over the goods and then jump over to the next store in town.

Education is key in what gets sold by sales staff. Nobody wants to look like an idiot in front of customers so they will avoid a complicated product when they see customers hovering around it. They want to avoid the tough questions. But different forms of training can get them presenting it. A lot of companies use online training now which is easy for you to provide details for. Some still use paper documents (newsletters, sales sheets etc) to do training or videos even. You just need to find out who in the company you need to talk to in order to get your training out to staff. This is a great topic to offer support on, and in many cases costs you nothing but some prep time on the content and you get sales staff talking to each customer about it.

Your goal is to make the training simple. Too often salespeople or product or marketing managers who deal in how many gigabytes, RAM, megapixels, watts or whatever other technical term on a daily basis throw all that language at the less technical people on the sales floor with training materials. In reality, these people are busy and have hundreds of other products to worry about so KEEP IT SIMPLE. The best way to do any quick training on a retail product is to give three key attributes of the product that are easy to remember. Your vacuum's key points may be:

A – Able to get into the smallest places

B – Backup battery for powerless places

C – Cleans better than any other vacuum on the market

Simple and effective – get them saying the ABC's of your product over and over and reward them with a token gift if they can repeat it back to you – now they have a story to tell the consumer when they see them floating around it, instead of bolting for the stockroom in fear.

Another powerful tool is the "sell what you own" plan where, if you can afford to do it, you give free samples or offer a really hot deal on a product you want them to push. If you sell twenty dollar headphones that actually look and sound better than the one hundred dollar ones, then a good move might be to give out a pair to a bunch of sales people in a store or at a training fair you may be attending. They will a) think you are awesome for giving them free things (everybody loves free stuff), b) have firsthand experience on how great they fit and sound and c) be able, with confidence, to tell the customers that these are a great pair of headphones and they know because they have a pair themselves. In this scenario – what if one hundred staff across twenty stores received a free pair, with a simple cheat sheet attached on the three top features of the product and the mandate from head office was that they needed to wear them every shift for one month...how great of a marketing tool would that be! You make the headphones for three dollars so it cost you three hundred dollars to likely sell a few thousand pairs that month.

Training fairs are amazing events most of the time. You want to jump on this opportunity if you can, as they do reach a lot of staff all in one place and in one to two days. These staff are usually hand-picked by store managers as the best candidates to get trained – likely because they are top sales people, work most often, show the most intelligence and potential or are superstars in some way. Retail is too expensive to run for companies to waste money paying hundreds of employees to fly to another city, stay in a hotel, eat and be entertained if they are on the list to be fired or deemed too dumb to comprehend the information they are going to get. You should assume your audience will be worth training and your investment in the event, big or small, will likely be a good investment. Get the details from the buyer or organizer and make an educated decision before signing up. Here are some tips:

- You may have no choice – some buyers need their top vendors training all their best products – if this is the case you should just find the money somewhere – it may be detrimental to decline and be the only non-supportive vendor
- Ask at the start of the year, when you are putting your plans together for spending with the buyer, if there are any training costs anticipated – make sure training, as it sometimes is, doesn't catch you by surprize and leave you scrambling for funding or forcing you to cut back other sales-driving programs
- Training often does not produce tangible, measurable results. It can - and that is important for making a decision the next time around on putting valuable back end dollars into it. Most of my experiences have been that they do add a lot of value and drive stronger sales – you just need to weigh this versus other activities you could spend money on – it's tough, but give it a fair value
- Dig into what the event is all about – how many are attending, who will be there, can they be given prizes for quizzes, what is the training format and most of all you want to know how much time you have to present to them.

Three hundred people from a one hundred store chain is a good amount of people to train for an investment of say five thousand dollars if you felt you would grow your sales by two hundred thousand dollars that year based on the value you place on the training of those people selling your product. But what if you dug into the event some more and found out that half of those people are store managers and not the sales people directly selling your product...not terrible, managers are good to woo too, but that knowledge may cut your sales lift calculation down to one hundred thousand dollars – still a fair lift for the event cost. Then you learn that they have invited all three of your main competitors to train on their product, so now the sales people are not really solely focussed on your sku when they go back to the stores – you may have to bribe them all to sway them to remember your pitch more. This is concerning now - and then finally you learn you will get just five minutes with six groups of fifty people – too little time to make an impactful speech and too large a group to remain interactive and keep everyone's attention. Now you realize it's perhaps not money well spent. You want to highlight your concerns to the buyer or organizer though – don't give up too quickly, they may very well take the feedback constructively and rearrange the event to allow for more time in smaller groups – I have seen it done.

When you or a company representative are at the event – make the most of every opportunity to get in front of the employees – sponsor a dinner or the entertainment of you can - give them something to remember you by. Be known as the presenter that was the funniest or most enjoyable, knowledgeable vendor – too often buyers get the negative feedback on events and the same people every year are given the "waste of my time, don't invite them next year" feedback. Don't be that vendor – you are wasting your and my valuable, potentially costly time with useless information, training materials that confuse or are incorrect or just simply being monotone and boring. It may be in your company's best interest to spring for a professional trainer if you need to – not every salesperson is also a polished speaker or skilled trainer.

Commission Sales Floors

Although not a lot of retailers are commission-based anymore, there are still some big national or regional majors or independents that have incented sales floors – mainly in the consumer electronics world. These retailers have an added dimension to their business and you need to understand this well if you are dealing with them.

A 'directed sales floor' (as it is often called) means the salespeople in the stores get a base pay plus a commission (usually in a percentage) for all or some products they sell. So Johnny makes ten dollars an hour and in one hour he sells a television for a thousand dollars and makes a ten percent commission. In that hour he made one hundred and ten dollars. There is also what is known as a 'spiff' – an additional dollar amount on a specific product the retailer wants to push above other products. Typically a vendor would support the spiff – covering all or some of the kick-back to the salesperson. There are usually rules to spiffed products – they need to be good products and they need to deliver strong margins or other advantages over competitive products on the floor. It would not be in the buyer's best interest to incent your product over others in their line-up if yours made less gross margin and made the salesperson look like an idiot if they are pushing your television, and for the same price the customer can clearly see there is another model beside it that is far superior – this makes the salesperson AND the retailer lose trust with the consumer.

The commission and spiff program is of great advantage to the vendor – if you can construct a strong plan with the buyer that rewards the salesperson you can get them shifting customers to your product consistently. This can significantly increase your sales - so do the math on what spiff support you can afford and what the sales lift will be. If your company makes five hundred dollars on every television you sell to a retailer and you kick in a twenty dollar spiff for each one sold by the salespeople on the floor, I would say it is money well spent if it nets you additional sales. If you make twenty dollars on a DVD player you sell to a retailer and it will take ten dollars to get them to shift the customer to your product versus the top selling brand, then the math just may not work out for you.

Also, getting the salespeople on the floor in your corner goes a long way – giving them free product to try so they can speak better to the benefits of the products, detailed training (because remember that they put food on the table by being able to explain products inside and out so feed them with knowledge – they want every bit they can get!), have sales contests, have store trainers visit them and schmooze them...make them your brand ambassadors! You want them telling customers that your television is the best there is (whether that's true or not) and showing every feature to the customer while ignoring the competitor's model – a good plan with the buyer can set this in motion and change your world.

If you don't have the ability to do any of the above, then you need to try to understand what your competitors are doing. Try to get one of the commission staff in the stores to spill the beans about their go-to products. You don't want to cross any lines and have it get back to the buyer, but make a buddy out in the stores and at the very least find out what specific products they get behind. It may be a simple as pretending to be a customer and seeing what they try to sell you when you ask them to recommend a television and a DVD player. Once you have done your spy mission you can put your plan together based on the competitors product – if it is lower priced you can either adjust your price or make a case to the buyer on why their salespeople should up-sell to yours based on a list of key benefits your product has over the competitor's model. If yours makes the buyer more top line and more bottom line dollars for their P&L in the end - then it is in their best interest to have the salespeople sell your stuff. Everyone is motivated by incentives – make sure the salesperson in the store wins and/or the buyer wins driving your products.

We have now decided on the product presentation and training while the product was en route to the stores (of course you would likely do this well in advance as part of the initial plan). Now that it is in my stores, on display, staff educated and ready to sell there are just a few quick follow-up points to double check, based on the previous chapter, to complete the cycle:

- Your ad plan is in place with the buyer and you are both ok with it
- You have ensured that your pricing and marketing plan with the buyer will not be crushed by the retailer's competitors or is not uncompetitive to what else is out in the market
- You weighed in on the forecast and it looks groovy, and have a plan to continually monitor it throughout the year to keep it on track
- You have some alternate plans if the sales slip and are no longer on forecast

- Your support plan is in place as to where your over and above dollars are going (and they are going to activities that don't waste your company's valuable cash)
- You have a strong plan established on the web to take advantage of the global shift to online shopping
- You have ensured your bosses are clear on your plans, and nobody will suddenly swoop in and scale back the plans you already promised the buyer
- You have regular follow-up meetings with the buyer to discuss current and potential future business
- You are keeping on top of market trends and what your competitors (and those of your buyer) are up to at all times – ready to shift plans if needed
- You are always seeing what your company can do to push sales of your product to retailers

Now you have covered my annual product cycle. You feel like you went twelve rounds with Mohammed Ali – but congratulations...you survived. Now you just have to prepare yourself to do it all over again. The good news is that you are much more prepared to slug it out another year. You know what all the moving parts are and how to make the most of them. Trust me – there are plenty more surprizes that will come your way, but hopefully I have covered a good portion of them. You may have people at your company who thankfully take care of things such as training and product demos, but you should still understand them and also make a call as to whether or not you actually NEED to do them (and if it's worth the money).

"Vendors need to understand how to leverage the systems to better understand Target's business and meet their core expectations. Basic mistakes can cause distrust for the teams at Target, and that can really hurt business. However, using the correct language and looking at business in the same way (sales etc) will be a key to success." - A former Senior Global Training Team Member for Target

"What I like to see in a sales rep is someone who is trying to work with you to accomplish a win-win scenario – because it is ideally a long-lasting relationship." – A Grocery Category Manager at Walmart

9

Ensure it Goes Smoothly

The buy-sell relationship is a rollercoaster that tries its best to throw you off the ride often through the experience. You CAN survive it with lots of hard work, intelligence, a strong stomach and good old fashioned luck. I have given you plenty of insight to help you stay on the ride a long time so far, but the following are some extra tips to help keep the relationship chugging along like a well-oiled machine.

Leveraging the Relationship

You are smart to use the relationship with one buyer to get through to another in the same company. Your company may sell products in multiple categories, and since you have already jumped through all the hoops and put in the long hours to successfully connect and start doing business there is nothing wrong with asking for an introduction with another potential business partner in the same company. Buyers wouldn't have any issue with this, but it's a little easier to do once you have some business under your belt with them because they can then recommend you and your product if they are happy with how things are going. There is a difference between sending an email to your salt buyer asking for the pepper buyers contact info and getting carbon copied on the intro email stating "see this guy's email below" versus "hey, I want to introduce you to one of my key vendors – we are doing some great business together..." The latter will help your case with landing listings in the pepper category much easier than having no push behind the introduction obviously.

I feel it better to get the contact via email for the above reason. A cold call doesn't always work well, and you take out the ability to leverage the buyer you work with now. A buyer really wants to know the success you can have on their floors, and if you can back it up with results from their own company you are that much further ahead.

Some buyers may really help you make the connection – you could always plead your case first as there is no harm in that. Let the buyer know you have another line of products that falls under another category and that it would really help you out if you could get an introduction to the buyer of that category. You can certainly ask them to give you a good recommendation if you feel it is warranted by the relationship and results you have had. If they are not comfortable with that I wouldn't push it – just get the contact details and when you get a hold of them, let them know you are already doing business in the building and, again – if warranted, let them know what you have done well for the company and invite them to speak to the buyer you deal with to back up your claims. If you are not sure you have done much to brag about or it's too early to tell - then avoid any claims that you have been a game-changer or revolutionized the other category.

Remind the buyer that your company having more business in the building only helps get brand awareness around the store – so customers are seeing Brand A's products in binders, notebooks and envelopes, so when they get to that buyer's category of pens and see the brand they recognize it and trust it. Also explain that the more purchases the buyer's company makes from you across multiple categories, the more overall money they can dip into to fund their programs

Trust

You need a buyer to trust you. You need them to feel comfortable around you and want to put their limited buying funds toward your product - because they don't get the sense you don't deserve the business or don't have any feelings they are going to regret the move to your company. How often do you hear of (or have experienced yourself) a case where a couple meet, start dating, and really hit it off, but one of them turns out to be a train wreck of a partner a couple months later. This happens all the time in buying – you think you have the great new vendor and you later get burned, or things just don't go as you planned. I buy my pink camera case from Brand A and a month later they screw up every order and delay the launch by a month because they have never been good at logistics. We have been burned enough to be sceptical of everyone, so you need to keep making sure we believe in you. Any signs that we are not in a partnership and our red flags start being raised.

Trust also comes from not feeling that a vendor thinks they are above you. Even if I buy for a tiny retailer in a small town in Kansas, you should still treat me like we are equals and not that I don't matter to you. If I think I mean nothing I will not trust that you have my best interests in mind.

"Vendors that are conceited and name drop send all the wrong messages," warns a Fashion Category Manager at Walmart. "This makes them hard to trust! Also, vendors that don't have their sh*t together are just too frustrating to bother with."

Take "no" Gracefully

There will be plenty of rejection in your life as a salesperson – perhaps more than acceptance – that is just the way it goes. It doesn't mean you are not a great salesperson, it just means that everyone doesn't need your products every time you pitch them.

Most buyers give much thought to their assortment decisions and often have other levels to pass their plans and decisions by - so if they say no to a product they mean one thing: NO. Upon hearing this, your next move should not be any of the following:

- Pleading with them unprofessionally to change their mind
- Throwing temper tantrums like a six year old
- Spitting in the buyer's face and calling them names
- Storming out of the meeting in anger

What you should do is:

- Acknowledge the decision and ask calmly if there is anything else you can do to change that decision – this gives you a last ditch chance to change the buyer's mind, while still giving the buyer a comfortable opportunity to reiterate the decision
- If you have an ace up your sleeve (say a further reduced cost you were holding out on) – this is the time to play that card, but it may still be a no
- Say "ok" and move on

If you feel it might help and not come across as sour grapes, you should let the buyer know any consequences that may arise from them saying no. If it is a hot deal you should let them know that that deal will then need to be offered to their competitors, as you need to unload the goods to someone. If it is a key product, you can reiterate that it will affect their sales and they may get beat in the market. Say these things with respect and as a side note so you do not come across as saying "you are an idiot for not buying this" – clearly that would not be a good thing.

Be the "Go-To" Vendor

In a lot of retail categories, buyers love to have that one vendor partner that can find the exact product they are looking for. This is tough to find and is usually a smaller vendor or distributor that is much more flexible, but it can be very lucrative and really help the relationship. For example, I'm the clock radio buyer for a big CE chain and I sell clock radios by a bunch of the top audio brands. I want a cheaper radio than the top tier brands that includes a special feature like nature sounds that nobody else is offering. I want someone to source this out domestically or find it in Asia, slap their name on it and sell it to me to fill my assortment needs. If I had a "go-to" partner that was flexible enough to pull these requests off (or at least come back to me and say it wouldn't work or be too costly so I can scratch it off my wish list) then that vendor partner becomes that much more valuable. Not everyone can be that partner, but if you have those sourcing skills then be sure you make the buyer fully aware of your capabilities.

Get it in Writing, and Don't Write it

Depending on how long you have been in the game, you probably already follow the rule that any big promise or deal with a buyer is best recapped in a printable, saveable and to-be-pulled-out-in-case-of-emergency email (if a letter signed in the buyer's own blood is not available). Not that you can't trust a buyer, but many things change over a week, month or year since you were told something - and if you feel it is that important to have back-up, you want to make sure you get it.

It is not always easy to ask for. Of course you want to avoid looking like you don't trust the buyer, but they should understand why you would want some proof of a plan. Say a buyer states they will give you four feet of counter space for twelve months in exchange for you paying one hundred thousand dollars to write off the other products currently in that section. You cut the cheque to the retailer and start planning what should go in that space. But what if that buyer leaves the company four months later and the new buyer doesn't think you are the right choice to have four feet of product in their assortment? In this situation you would a) hope that they take your word for it that you paid for twelve months, b) hope the old buyer's boss recalls the deal or c) you have a beautiful 8.5 x 11 sheet of paper as back-up from the buyer detailing the agreement. Better safe than sorry.

Many retailers, in this lean and mean financial world we live in today, are hiring auditors to scan through the books and various emails hunting for errors and missed monies. In this case you want to ensure that YOUR emails do not make any promises or incorrect statements. You want to stick to facts, and your emails should only recap activity that is actually going to occur. If it does not materialize – send a follow-up email with the original attached stating that the activity did not happen. It may not be necessary – you can clarify what processes the retailer has with the buyer to be sure. If they do have the team of circling sharks on payroll, be sure to cover yourself – they WILL find that random email promising money that never came to fruition and make a claim against you to try to squeeze some money out of you – it is what they are paid to do and they are good at it. A lot of times they leave it to your company to disprove the claim, which can be done - but is a bunch of unnecessary work for you or your accounting team.

Even without auditors you should avoid putting yourself and your company in an awkward spot from what is written in an email. Emails can be misunderstood or can be used against you. It is extremely rare that an email or letter between buyer and vendor ends up being used in legal action but it is a concern – you never know what can happen, so it is best to talk in person or over the phone when it comes to major deals or scenarios with financial implications until they are one hundred percent agreed upon – in which case you can recap the deal on email.

Escalating

There are always situations that arise in your job where you need to either go to your boss for help or go above the buyer to their boss to push something through. These are obviously always tough situations – you don't want to anger your buyer as they are the ones making the day to day product decisions and can make your life difficult if you rub them the wrong way. There are many reasons for escalating but you want to always be sure the benefits outweigh the risks of alienating your buyer. These are some examples:

You are short purchases to make your year and the buyer has no dollars open to buy	Escalating may be seen as you not taking the buyer's word for it that they are tapped out of open to buy dollars – you should ask the buyer first if you could escalate this to try to get the buyer more funds or let them know how important it is and that you need to get your boss involved. This one should never come across as looking like the buyer let you down, as this an over and above partnership request

The buyer was rude, inappropriate or offensive to a level that is unacceptable	This is a great time to express your concerns to a higher level on your side and that of the retailer. Some buyers are very tough to deal with and you need to be sure the behavior is above and beyond acceptable levels before going down that path - because that buyer will be even angrier once they get ratted out and it may make your interactions that much tougher going forward
The buyer is sloppy with how they manage the business and how they manage your product	Again, this is open to interpretation – you need to have concrete examples of how they have mismanaged the business before you get them in trouble – always ask yourself if escalating situations is worth it
The buyer does not respond to your emails or phone calls	Try to find a way to communicate that works for both parties first. Send an email asking why you cannot seem to get a hold of them easily – if they ignore that and you have been ignored for a week or longer then yes, escalate.
Repeated pleading or warning on a subject does not change the buyer's behavior	For example: you have an embargo date on a DVD launch (a "not to be put out before" date) and a buyer breaks that, they should be warned that they have to adhere to the street dates. If they do it again on the next big release then they are just not playing by the rules and it is causing your company pain – this needs to be escalated
You want more product listings so you think presenting to the buyers boss will help	Your primary relationship is with the buyer NOT their boss. If you have presented to the buyer and they said no, turning to the buyer's boss to try to get them to force the buyer to bring it questionable. You can certainly request to plead your case further with the buyer and his boss, but avoid skipping over the buyer completely – it may work, but the buyer will not be a big fan of yours

Before You Hit Send

It has happened to me several times in the past decade – the email sent my way, by accident or not, that the salesperson regrets hitting the send button on. It has happened to all of us, and it is a huge source of panic and anxiety. I realize you have a million things going on, but always step back, take a deep breath and do the two-second scan of your email before you send it. This is what you want to look for:

- Is it addressed to the proper person at the right company?

- Do I want all the people it's going to reading this?

- Could this get you or the buyer in hot water?

- Is it privileged information you maybe shouldn't be sharing?

- Does it contain a trail of previous emails you don't want other people reading?

- Does it open you up to commitments you shouldn't be making?

What is the tone of your email? This is one of the downfalls of email versus phone communication – you cannot always know how your wording gets taken by the reader. Often a joke or sarcastic comment comes across as a rude statement that could do serious damage to your relationship, and sometimes your attempts to back-peddle or explain it just make you look more guilty. Often the recipient will never tell you they were taken aback by your comment and will just forever hold a grudge. If you are trying to lighten things up with a joking statement

ALWAYS toss in a "(just kidding," happy face, or LOL after it – never leave it to chance that your buyer will take it the right way.

BOLDING SENTENCES IS POWERFUL BUT ALSO READS AS YELLING. Exclamation points are also valuable in getting a point across, but can also signal anger! Question marks on a statement come across often as you being confused about something as opposed to inquisitive or throwing out a thought starter for everyone to weigh in on perhaps?

Unfortunately your email may be judged – it represents you and your company. If it is sloppy with bad spelling, horrible grammar, incorrect information or any of the above issues, the buyer and anyone else on the email list will think of you as perhaps being messy, uneducated, unprofessional, rude or even a liability - so take your emails seriously and double check them before pushing the button to the world.

The Closing Techniques

There are several different closing techniques used by salespeople in this business. It depends on how they were trained, who they were trained by, or who they looked up to when they were learning the ins and outs of the sales profession. I personally prefer to deal with newer salespeople, as they often don't have what I consider to be old-school techniques. These sales tactics can be effective on a lot of buyers and should be in a salesperson's repertoire, but like many other pieces of the puzzle - you need to understand who you are dealing with before you use them.

The "hard close" is a method where you pitch someone on a product and at the end you essentially shove it down their throat, back them into a corner and attempt to give them no choice but to buy it. This is less tolerated in today's buying world in a lot of categories because never has there been so much choice of products and partners - and a lot of them hungry for business. The hard close can seem like bullying or desperation to some, so use it only when you know it's going to work. It really is a last resort closing technique.

The "assumptive close" is another gem that has been used forever. With this style the salesperson pitches the product like there is no question you are going to buy it and proceeds like you had committed to it from the very beginning. This is an interesting one when people pull it out – because it really can come across as arrogance and paints the stereotypical picture of a used car salesman (which some buyers label any 'slimy' salespeople they don't like). It can be effective, but you have to be really good at it to use it.

Most buyers honestly see right through these things – at least ones that have been around a while. You have to remember that along with more choice there is also less money to make purchases and fewer customers in tougher economic times - so buyers scrutinize every product and plan to make sure it is the right one. Less often will you be able to steer a buyer into the purchase or pull a fast one on them. Times have changed.

Buyers want to have open dialog and hammer out a suitable game plan. They will buy what makes sense to them (not to say they are always necessarily correct) and reject what doesn't. Having said that there are still good, effective ways to close the sale:

- The win-win scenario – presenting a plan that shows how both parties can come away with big sales and healthy profits will usually work best. Show the buyer why this is in their best interest to accept the pitch and play to their needs (as detailed in several parts of the book already)

- The incredibly detailed plan – some of it may be smoke and mirrors, but if you show you have done your homework and researched every last bit of the buyer's business to come up with the perfect plan you can often win over the buyer with your efforts and arguments and put yourself ahead of other vendors who didn't do all the work. A strong presentation is key here as well

- Catering to what the buyer most needs – if you can convince the buyer that THEY influenced the plan you presented to them because of their comments and requests you can sway them to agree to what you might have been pitching all along. Make them feel really good about the plan and praise their actual (or pretend) contributions to keep them thinking it was something they always wanted. This is a little different from the assumptive close and works much better

- Let the buyer use the product themselves in the case of new technologies, electronic gadgets and other such products. What better way to let them see how great a product is and how much their customer base needs it than to get them hooked on how great and indispensable it is

Avoid the bullying or backing the buyer into the corner – it does not sit well with us. If I say I don't like your new no-slip sock line then what makes you think I'm going to change my mind two minutes later when you ask me for the fourth time if I am going to take the line? Or when I am in a meeting or at a dinner with a bunch of people from your company and multiple people question my decision to not carry a product or keep asking how I could think it wasn't the best sock ever made. I already said no, so why keep pounding away at me – I certainly won't change my mind in this situation. You are best to revisit it at another time or change something to convince me - like better margin or fixing something I said I didn't like.

If I say no you definitely have the right to ask me to clarify why I didn't like the product or why I don't believe it fits my assortment. By doing this you get a list of things to improve upon and come back to me with when you try to re-pitch it. If I say it would be a great product if the socks didn't slip down my leg all the time, as they did when I tested them out, and you come back a few weeks later with tighter leg bands - then it is a lot harder for me to say no. If I say no because they just don't fit into my plans and there is no opening to go back at it right now, then don't beg and plead or ask ten more times why not – this is just sad and annoying – deal with rejection better and learn to move on.

There is no real set timeline I can recommend for you to wait before pitching that same product again to me, but if you do you better have a new game plan. Just re-pitching the same product in the same way is ridiculous since it didn't work the first time - so make sure you can offer it in a different way, and give enough time between pitches to not seem desperate or pushy. Keep an eye out in my assortment and out in the market for changes – perhaps that product that beat yours out gets dropped by the buyer, the manufacturer kills it, or you get the gift of a damaging recall on their product which allows you to swoop in and get yours in the assortment.

Tell No Lies

Here's a little tip for you: most buyers know when you are lying. You have to remember that we get paid to negotiate, build relationships, drive sales and protect the business. In protecting the business we need to filter through the lies, underhandedness and general BS. It disappoints me when a salesperson lies to my face and I know they are lying. It greatly brings down my respect and trust of them and their company. Does this mean you should never bend the truth? Actually, no – everyone plays with the truth to get what they want and I don't suggest you abandon this tactic - but you need to be very tactful in doing it and make sure I can't call you on it. Here are some examples:

- "We put this product up on the (competitor).com website and the sales were phenomenal!" – were they really? Define phenomenal – this over-exaggeration is common, but not bought by the buyer unless you have something to back up your claim

- "We can get it to you from Asia within a week" – we all know NOTHING gets out of Asia, through customs and turned around in a week without miracles...why make such a bold claim just to guarantee you will let me down – it's a bad way to do business and even worse if we are meeting for the first time

- "Our products are the best" – never make this claim unless you hands down kill every other product in your category by a country mile. This sentence can open you up to criticism from the buyer or a tearing apart of your product's features versus what the buyer may feel is a better one they have seen. You are better off going humble and changing it to "our products are some of the best in the market"

- "We have thousands of followers who love our products on Facebook" – buyers are familiar with Facebook and other social media, and we know that all it takes to get fans on these platforms is a product giveaway or a booth at a tradeshow soliciting sign-ups, so don't try to convince a buyer these people are true lovers of the product who have used it and stand behind it (in some cases this may be true of course)

- "Trust me, I won't let you down" – no, trust me when I say I don't trust you until I really know you and you have gained my trust, so don't stand behind your reputation until you have one established with the buyer. This does not mean I think you are misrepresenting yourself, but early on you may want to phrase it as "you will see over time that I am not in the business of letting people down" – in fact, that is a great reassuring statement to use when building a relationship with a buyer - as trust is paramount in our business

Packaging

Obviously the way your product looks on the shelf is a major key to selling it, but a lot of times I am shocked at what I see. There are different schools of thought out there when it comes to what packaging should represent:

121

- I can't afford nice packaging so I am going to make this one hundred dollar item look like it is ten dollars
- The packaging should be like the greatest gift anyone has ever opened
- The package should be informative but simple, and represent the product that is inside

Of course you would assume the third one is what most people would gravitate toward, but that isn't always the case. The first point, the cheapo route, is common unfortunately. If you are going to cut corners on something as important as the packaging – think twice. You can be cost effective but still professional. Spend the extra five cents a pack on glossy cardboard, get a professional team to design the package and graphics and get opinions from professionals (including the buyer) on what it should say on it. We look at hundreds of products and packages in a year and also have customer and store feedback behind us – we can give very good feedback to help you (and if we buy it, help us).

The second point is a frustrating one. We all agree a high-end product of any kind needs packaging that reflects the value and quality of what is inside, but I have seen plenty of beautiful packages get in the way of the ultimate goal: selling the product! Some common mistakes in over-producing the package include:

- No visibility to the product inside – say it is a pair of five hundred dollar headphones – unless they are the have-to-have headphones of the year and people just come in and buy them sight unseen, you can't just have a really nice box with a name on it or even just a picture of the product. That customer is going to wear them around in public – it's a fashion accessory, so they need to see them live to know they will love them for their hard-earned five hundred bones. You can still have professional packaging and still put a window on the box

- Not enough product details – Apple created a world where a simple, elegant white box with minimal writing on it was considered amazing, but since your product hasn't changed the world like theirs has you can't get away with it. Customers want to know all about what they are buying, but have short attention spans so it can be tricky. As a rule of thumb you give consumers twenty seconds to garner as much information as possible from your packaging. If you are selling a toaster they need to know some key details: brand, how many slices it does at one time, what settings it has, if it has a crumb tray and what color it is so it can be matched to the kitchen décor or appliance colors. You can easily fit this on a few bullet points on the front of the box. QR codes are being put on more packages these days which can be scanned on a smartphone to pull up your web page and get additional information about a product so you don't have to put everything on the box
- Not secure – theft is a major concern for retailers, so if you have a really fancy package but it unfolds in five seconds flat so a thief can grab the product and shove it in their pocket, it is not going to work well in stores. Secure packaging is a must in many categories – make sure you know the expectations of yours
- Lack of sturdiness – it's great that you made a pretty package, but does the cardboard tab that allows it to

hang from my store pegs tear off from the weight of the package? Does the box dent or scuff really easily so it looks like it was bought second hand by the time it gets brought to the floor and put on the shelf? These are things you need to look at during packaging design as any damaged packaging, even if the product is fine inside, deters purchasers

The optimal route is the last point discussed at the beginning of this section – informative (just enough product details for the customer to make an educated decision), simple (should not be hard on the eyes, should attract the shopper) and represent the product inside. Don't over-dress a simple or low-end product. Don't try to make a ten dollar product look like a one hundred dollar one - but you should try to make it look like a twenty dollar item. You want to manage people's expectations to avoid returns and bad PR. On the flip side, you want the packaging on the one hundred dollar item to look like it's worth it – you wouldn't put thousand dollar real diamond cufflinks in plastic clam packaging and peg them (at least I hope not). The buyer is going to judge your product, and that includes how it is packaged - so make sure it is professional. If it is just a mock-up package make sure you explain it is not final, and if you want their honest feedback or just want to make them feel like they are contributing to the product development – just ask!

There are so many facets of the buying game – it's a wonder either of us gets to go home and see our families at the end of the day (some days we don't!). You need to make note of all these points and check them off as you triple check that each is in place. One of these going south could destroy all the hard work you did on the rest of them. I know this does sound like quite a challenge, and likely it wouldn't be the case, but at the end of the day the message is this: cover all the bases and don't let any of them slip. There are many moving parts – keep them running smoothly!

"A Challenge was when vendors were not communicative when anything happened. Early communication of challenges or opportunities helps Target to make better business decisions, and make the vendor more of a true partner." – A former Senior Global Training Team Member for Target

"The biggest pet peeve for me is a vendor who never knows when to quit trying to bring something in when you said no already." – A Grocery Category Manager at Walmart

Conclusion

There you have it – a long laundry list of do's and don'ts, and a rare view into the world of the buyer. By understanding what happens on the other side of the desk you can leverage this knowledge to be a better salesperson and close the buyer easier. It will give you the insight to create better plans, spend money more wisely, drive more sales and create longer-lasting and stronger relationships with your buyers and their teams. Take all this information with a grain of salt of course, but by looking at the relationship in a different way you can maximize it and create advantage for yourself from this new knowledge.

It is a mental game, like chess. It is a game where you will always have to watch what you say, what you do and how you interact with the buyers, their teams and even your teams. Most salespeople go in to the gig with no real knowledge of how it all works and what they should be doing for success. They may learn as they go and possibly have a great mentor to teach them what they know, but rarely do they truly understand the ins and outs of the entire equation...which you can see is very complex from what you have read. In the past you may have said "why would I need to know how a buyer's P&L works?" or "the buyer has a decent forecast...I'm just going with what they have." You now know that there are multiple wins available to you by understanding such things – how they work and why they are in place. Seize the opportunity to take your game to the next level.

The more you talk to your buyers, the more you can understand their needs and goals and what makes them tick (or what stresses them out). It is always a work in progress, and you may never come across the perfect buyer in your mind, but you may be able to make your life a lot more pleasant both professionally and personally with less stress and more commissions. Being in buying and being in sales are not jobs for the faint of heart – they are demanding and pressure-filled jobs, so taking advantage of new ways of looking at selling - which can open up a lot of doors and make you the best at what you do. At least that is the aim of this book – now go out, put these things into practice and...close me if you can.

Acknowledgements

I would like to thank all my employers, co-workers, suppliers and long-time professional friends for getting me to where I am today. I would also like to thank the many buyers from all over North America who generously contributed their knowledge to this valuable project to help retail salespeople and others in their pursuit of perfection.

Most of all I would like to thank my wife and kids for all their support and love over the years. Retail is NOT an easy profession – it means long days, working from home, lots of travel and some grumpy periods when things aren't going as planned. You guys have always stuck by me, and I have achieved great results in my career because of that dedication and support.

Thank you for buying this book. It was a fun project to work on as a writer and as a professional. I know some spots may sound either way too basic or a bit harsh at times, but my goal was to not let any detail slide – it may be valuable to somebody at some point in time and if I have helped just one of my fellow warriors in this bloody battle called retail – I have succeeded.

Thomas Spago

tomspago@yahoo.com

Please contact the agency for retail consulting services with Thomas and a multitude of top buyers from across North America.

www.ingramcontent.com/pod-product-compliance
Lightning Source LLC
Chambersburg PA
CBHW022006170526
45157CB00003B/1168